BODY BELIEFS

Women, Weight Loss, and Happiness

by

Jason Seib

TELEMACHUS PRESS

BODY BELIEFS

Cover design by Telemachus Press, LLC

Cover art © Copyright iStock Photo/467943148/briddy

Published by Telemachus Press, LLC
http://www.telemachuspress.com

ISBN# 978-1-945330-42-1 (paperback)

SELF-HELP / Motivational & Inspirational

Version 2017.06.13

TABLE OF CONTENTS

BODY BELIEFS

Women, Weight Loss, and Happiness

Acknowledgements

Nothing about this creation of this book happened in a vacuum. These are the people who helped me. Words cannot express my gratitude, but I will try.

Sheryl, you are my strength.

Liesel, Capri, and Daphne, you are my reason.

Robert Biswas-Diener, you helped me brainstorm nearly every concept in the book. Without you to challenge me and make me think in new ways, I'd be years behind where I am now.

Erica, you grease the wheels of my career and I have learned so much through your experience.

Kris, you are a pillar of strength and consistency as my friend and business partner.

Robb Wolf, I couldn't write another book without thanking you again. I'm on this path in large part because of your teaching and example.

Sarah Fragoso, we learned so much together. I miss you.

Julie Van Keuren, you're an amazing editor and far too kind to me.

To all the women I have worked with in my career, thank you for sharing your struggles with me and trusting me to help you. You taught me so much and I hope you benefitted as much from knowing me as I have from knowing you.

INTRODUCTION

Jenny's Story

Jenny was 6 when she learned that fat was bad. She was pretending to be a kitty, crawling on all fours and meowing as she made her way into her parents' room, where she found her mother standing in front of the mirror with a disgusted look on her face and both hands pinching the fat on her belly.

"What are you doing, Mommy?" Jenny asked. "Nothing, sweetie," her mother said with a sigh. "Mommy is just fat."

Jenny was confused. Her mother was the most beautiful woman she knew, but apparently there was something wrong with being able to pinch your stomach. Jenny pinched her own stomach and wondered if there was something wrong with her, too, but she mostly just felt proud to be like her mom.

As Jenny got older, she was always aware that her mother was not happy in her own skin. The lesson Jenny took from her mother's poor body image was that women should always worry about how they look, and especially about the number they see on their bathroom scale. Jenny would occasionally stand on her mother's scale, but she had no frame of reference or any reason to feel bad about herself, so she didn't put a lot of stock in what she was doing. She just wanted to be a big girl, and big girls weighed themselves and talked about their weight a lot.

Then it happened. One day when Jenny was 11, she wore a brand new black-and-white dress to school. She felt so proud of the way she looked, and she beamed when one of her friends noticed her dress and gave her a compliment. Seeing the exchange, a boy named Joseph saw a chance, as kids often do, to get some attention by taking a jab at a classmate. "You actually like Jenny's dress?!" he yelled. "She looks like a fat dairy cow!" Jenny was mortified as Joseph ran off laughing with two other boys. Decades later, she would still remember every detail of that moment, right down to the smell of the fresh-cut grass on the playground.

Two years later, Jenny was 13 and cute as a button, but she wasn't a tiny girl. In fact, she was the "biggest" of her two best friends, but that was only because they were exceptionally small. When puberty arrived, it brought with it an interest in boys and an acute awareness of the bodies around her. Sadly, Jenny's mom had taught her that size matters—a lot. Jenny compared her body with those of her friends on a daily basis and almost always felt worse each time.

Jenny's father was a good man who loved her mother deeply, but his opinions never seemed to matter when it came to her mom's body image. He had been beaten down by the slow realization that, regardless of how much he fawned over her, his wife would always hate her body. By the time Jenny was old enough to notice such things, he was beyond trying and wasn't setting a great example of male attraction anymore. To make matters worse, he was a typical male and, although he never meant an ounce of harm, he wasn't always as sensitive as daughters sometimes need dads to be. Comments like "Maybe you shouldn't eat so much, honey" would stick in Jenny's mind forever.

Jumping ahead to her senior year in high school, Jenny was carrying what she estimated to be an extra 15 pounds of fat. It was actually more like 8 extra pounds, but she wanted so badly to be one of the "skinny girls." She hadn't yet had a serious boyfriend, and she was positive that this was because she was fat.

In her second year of college, Jenny let her guard down and dated a jackass named Jeff. When she caught Jeff cheating on her, he did what most scumbags do and tried to hurt her on his way out the door in an attempt to justify his behavior and convince himself that he hadn't just lost a wonderful girl. "You're fat and I always knew I could do better than you!" He screamed it loud enough for Jenny's neighbors to hear. She cried for two weeks while she starved herself so she could "make him eat those words!"

After a few more bad picks, Jenny finally found herself married to a wonderful guy named Scott who regularly told her she was the most beautiful woman in the world. Each time he said it, Jenny would think, "He's too kind to tell me that I'm fat, but I'm sure he thinks it." Her insecurities drained her husband the same way her mother's insecurities drained her father. Scott eventually became frustrated with her and the casual way she disregarded his opinions, but Jenny misinterpreted his frustration as dissatisfaction with her body and proof that she had been right all along.

With each failed weight-loss attempt, the temporary losses would be undone by slightly more weight regained than what she had lost in the first place. Each "failure" would mar her psyche and whittle away a little more of her self-worth and confidence.

When she looks around her world now, Jenny sees mountains of evidence clearly indicating that she would finally be happy if she could only make her body look good. From Jenny's vantage point, everyone else *clearly* dislikes the way she looks, and the good looking people are *clearly* happier than she is.

Thus unfolds the all-too-common life of a perpetual dieter. Jenny's body is her enemy. She hates it for how it looks. She hates it for not doing what she wants it to do each time she tries a new weight-loss trick. She hates it for being the reason she has never been truly happy. And she hates it for constantly occupying her thoughts. What has she done to deserve this?

~~~~

Jenny's story is a loose representation of what an uncountable number of women are living out each day in the Western world. The details come in lots of flavors—abusive parents, siblings who torture for fun, and eating disorders, just to name a few—but the results are the same. It may seem hard to believe right now, but it is most definitely psychology and perspective, not the step-by-step process of fat loss, that keeps women from achieving the goals they set for themselves in an effort to change their bodies for the better.

I know it's a bold statement, but if you give me a fair chance, this book will change the way you look at your body and weight loss forever. I'm not promising that I can magically make you happy in your own skin, but I truly believe that I can set you on that path. This is not the typical self-help cheerleading drivel that is guaranteed to make you feel good for a minute while never eliciting any real change in you. We're going to talk about a lot of things that you've probably never considered before, and some of those things are going to sting a bit. It will certainly never be my intention to hurt your feelings, but I can't candy-coat this stuff for you. Sometimes tough love will be my only option. *Please* stay with me. I *really* want to help you.

"Who does he think he is?"

It's true, I'm a man. Some women will say, "Why in the hell would I ever let a *man* tell me how I should think about my body? No man knows what it's like to be a woman!"

I can't contest that statement, but I hope you'll at least allow me to explain how I came to be where I am today and how I acquired my unique knowledge and perspective. I honestly believe I can help you, as I have already helped so many, and I think you'll find that my motives are pure.
First and foremost, I'm a devoted husband to my wonderful wife, Sheryl, and a father to three little girls, Liesel, Capri, and Daphne. Those little ladies are the reason my world turns, and I will do anything and everything in my power to help them escape the path that Jenny took.

Second, I'm a fat-loss coach. I teach proper nutrition, fitness, sleep, and stress management in my gym, in the other books I've written, in my online communities, and through consulting. My clients and followers are approximately 90 percent female, and most are frustrated yo-yo dieters who have done lots of desperate things to try to lose weight and find some level of happiness with their bodies. It was quite a few years ago when I realized that the overwhelming majority of my job was about heads, not bodies. In recent years, I've found what I believe to be indisputable proof of this.

After a couple of decades of learning, I created a fat-loss diet called AltShift, and I felt like all my dreams had come true. I finally had something that worked. I mean *really* worked! Everyone we tested AltShift on got amazing results, and once we released it to the public, even more amazing stories than I ever could have imagined began to pour in. We were getting people the results they wanted, and we were doing it without ever detracting from overall health or starving anyone, which meant we were producing sustainable results.

Wait! Hold on there! Don't go running off to find AltShift just yet.

Despite the fact that AltShift was doing everything I ever hoped a diet would do, people were also *failing* in droves. Many would get amazing results while telling us how easy everything was for them, only to quit and disappear for a while. Some of these people would come back later and tell us how they had no idea why they stopped. Others would say they sabotaged themselves and just couldn't get back on the wagon. Nobody said it was because AltShift was too hard to maintain.

Many other people would see all the results we were producing and hear the people in our communities talking about how easy their results were coming, but they would never really be able to get fully within compliance. Every few days, or maybe every few weeks, they would stumble and ruin all their hard work with a bunch of junk food. We could hear their frustration in their complaints and pleas for support as they redoubled their efforts to try again, but the cycle would almost always repeat itself.

Another fraction would rationalize that if they applied partial effort, they should see partial results. When I explained that health and fat loss are all about adaptation to a new lifestyle and new health inputs, and that adaptation doesn't happen to bodies that are receiving mixed signals, these people would usually quit trying. Going all in was simply more than they could handle.

There are plenty of other similar scenarios, but as you can see, these are problems of psychology and perspective. Body image, self-efficacy, extrinsic motivations, external loci of control, and so many other mental factors that we'll discuss in this book were the real culprits.

I found myself surrounded by women like Jenny who were saying to me, "I don't like myself very much. I don't have a lot of self-worth or self-confidence. I turn away every time I see myself in a mirror. I believe that I'm not like those other women who have great bodies. I'm always suspicious of compliments. I don't truly believe that I have the power to change. When I meet new people, I always assume that they think I'm fat. The real reason I want to change the way I look is so that other people will like me more. Now: Help me solve all these problems by telling me how many carbs I should eat each day!"

When I break it down like this, I'm hoping you can see how silly it is for someone with this perspective to expect long-term success. It's just not going to happen. Even with a protocol that might be perfect in an emotional and psychological vacuum, this woman cannot succeed because she will always get in her own way.

So, after what I learned from AltShift, this book became a mandatory project for me. I have already figured out how to help people lose weight; now I need to help them get to the starting line with real potential to finish the race. I've been beating this drum for years, but I've never taken the time to put everything I know about proper fat loss perspective in one place until now. This book is all about beliefs: the false assumptions you're probably making about your body, weight loss, attraction, and so many other related subjects, as well as all the things you'll need to believe wholeheartedly in order to stop yo-yo dieting and create sustainable results that you can keep for a lifetime. I'm going to show you all those things—the good, bad, and the ugly—and I'm going to do everything I can to help you *truly* believe them so that you can *truly* implement them.

One last point before we begin. My message is not "Just love yourself the way you are." I honestly believe that's a pipe dream that spawns from apathy. My message is and will always be "Love yourself enough to change for the right reasons."

Let's get started, shall we?

Chapter One
My Job Is a Joke, but Not a Funny One

I'VE CHOSEN TO to spend my life teaching people how to be healthy and fit. As such, I'm doing something that would have been completely unnecessary for nearly all of the past 2.6 million years, as selective pressures shaped our species into what it is today. I need to dig into a little science here to make a point, but never fear: This section is not setting the tone for the rest of the book. This is an important part of the foundation for healthy fat-loss beliefs, though, so please bear with me.

I know your mom told you that you're a unique little snowflake, but we are really just animals. Apes, to be precise, but let's jump to something more elegant and use tigers as an example. If a tiger lives in an environment that can sustain her, with plenty of food, water, and just the right number of other tigers, she will typically be a healthy tiger. In other words, when tigers live in the world to which they are well-adapted, the default outcome is health. It's the same for all animals. That's just the way evolution works. Life adapts to niches, and adaptation allows for thriving.

The same is absolutely true for humans. Unfortunately for us, though, we're too smart for our own good and have altered our environment. We've dramatically changed the kinds of foods we have available to us, as well as the amount of movement that is required for us to acquire that food. In fact, we all used to have the same job description: food acquisition. And this is where things get interesting.

When we remember that we all used to be hunter-gatherers, and that we lived that way for a *very* long time, it starts to get easy to figure out why we're so overweight in the Western world. No, it's not because food was scarce and life was very hard, so we were all skinny little wretches. Those are ridiculous concepts that have never been supported by anthropology, and you should put them out of your mind forever. In reality, there are a couple of major environmental changes that are smashing our health and vitality. And, sadly, we will never evolve to deal with these things.

The first part of this conundrum we find ourselves in is that we are hardwired to find food and then sit down and rest. This basic concept is called "optimal foraging strategy," and it affects all animals. The gist is that we should rarely pass up easily accessible calories in favor of calories that are harder to acquire. That would just be wasteful. When your only job is to find some food, there's no point in working harder than necessary.

The second part is about flavor. We actually developed a sense of taste to help us find nutrition in nature, not so that we could experience ecstasy every time we eat. When a food tastes good, we get a dopamine response in our brains. Dopamine is a *wanting* hormone, not a liking hormone, and its job is to make us repeat things. Since we evolved in a world where flavor was always correlated to nutritional value (the better something tasted, the greater the nutritional value), this flavor-reward system was very helpful in altering our behavior to make sure that we developed healthy eating habits. In short, if something was yummy, we could be assured that it was good for us, and dopamine would encourage us to eat it again often.

Okay, so let's take our hunter-gatherer ancestors and propel them into modern times without changing their genetics in any significant way, which is exactly what happened to us. We now live in a world where flavor is often not even remotely correlated to nutrition, food is so readily available that virtually none of us spend any real time finding it each day, and most of us have outsourced nearly all the movement that we used to have to do just to stay alive.

Think about it like this: When you're staring down the barrel of a cupcake, every physiological and biochemical response in your body is telling you that the correct decision is to eat the cupcake, see if there are more cupcakes that you can eat, and then chill out for a while and enjoy having a full belly. Everything in you that evolved to help you find food and stay alive in nature is convinced that this cupcake is a dream come true. It tastes good so it *must* be good for you. In fact, until a moment ago in our long evolutionary history, there was no such thing as food that was "bad" for you.

If you hope to sidestep the temptations of the cupcake, you have to use your prefrontal cortex, a tiny part of our brains behind our foreheads that developed only very recently in the context of our evolution. This is where you'll find the willpower to push back against those oldest of human systems, flavor and food reward. In other words, you are innately programmed to eat the cupcake, but you must cognitively, diligently, and purposefully override those innate drives in order to not eat the cupcake.

If you're still with me, this means it's not you that is broken, it's our world. If you got fat in this modern environment, you're a huge evolutionary success. To demonstrate that I'm not just trying to throw you a bone here, I asked Robb Wolf, my friend and the author of two amazing books, *Wired to Eat* and *The Paleo Solution*, to share his thoughts on this subject. He corroborated my points, saying this:

> Optimal foraging strategy worked kind of like a bank account. We had to spend less than we made or we ended up bankrupt. Historically, we had to get more than we

gave up, and we're wired for that, but now it's almost impossible to create a situation in which we can't get more than we need. It's a strategy that economically explains why so many people are overweight.

This brings us back to the fact that my job is a joke. Whenever I stop to think about it, I'm reminded that I spend a great deal of my life teaching people how to create something that should have happened by accident. Literally not one of us should ever have to think about fitness and nutrition. For our ancient ancestors, if it was called "food," then it was good for them. And can you imagine telling someone 20,000 years ago that you were going to go for a walk in a big circle and end up right back where you started without doing or getting anything? And what about resistance training?

"Hey Og, I'm going to go pick up that heavy rock over and over again and then leave it right where I found it."

"Sounds good! We'll just kill you in your sleep since you're clearly crazy enough to be a danger to all of us. Have fun, though!"

All joking aside, this is the stuff you need to think about whenever you find yourself scowling at your reflection. Your body did not betray you. On the contrary, it did everything it was programmed to do to keep you alive and kicking. You are an amazing biochemical machine. Unfortunately, you are a machine that was built for an environment quite different from the one you live in.

Yes, the circumstances suck, but your body deserves your love and compassion, not your hatred and abuse. It didn't do anything wrong. It simply responded to the inputs you gave it, and you gave it those inputs because they made perfect sense to your biology. There is no need to place blame, and negative emotions needn't be part of this story. You're learning now, and that's all that matters.

Less hate and torture, more love and nurture.

Chapter Two
Long-Term Goal Setting

AS I CONTINUED to apply an evolutionary lens to my observations of fat loss, another thing that began to niggle at the back of my mind was that humans don't seem to be hardwired for long-term goals. I ended up at this conclusion after trying and failing to think about a long-term goal that our hunter-gatherer ancestors might have set for themselves. There was nothing to save, because hunting and gathering usually requires a lot of moving around, so too many possessions would be a pain in the rear, and food could not be stored. Since there was nobody with a different career than you, there would be nothing to "buy" with an accumulated amount of something valuable. Anything that looked like trade would have happened with today's spoils.

There was also nothing to lose, like body fat, because overweight and obese bodies are quite rare in hunter-gatherers, being predominantly a product of modern society. A person could potentially want to get better at something, like hunting, but I doubt that a long-term goal with specific parameters would ever have been set. For example, I don't think anyone would have said something like, "I want to be able to shoot a 4-inch group of arrows from 30 yards by May 28." Instead, that person would probably just hunt and practice each day.

I eventually had the opportunity to ask for a professional opinion on my hypothesis. John Medina, developmental molecular biologist and author of the amazing New York Times best-seller *Brain Rules*, was gracious enough to have lunch with me and a couple of my police officer friends so that we could pick his brain about brains. I was humbled by his kindness and willingness to help us in exchange for nothing more than a steak salad. When I told him that I thought humans were not hardwired for long-term goal setting, he said, "That's true. We are all about immediate gratification. We had to be for survival."

It all makes perfect sense. When we're hot, we should be looking for a way to cool off. When we're cold, we should be looking for a way to get warm. When we're hungry, we need food. When we're thirsty, water needs to be a priority.

What does this mean for us? Unfortunately, it means that wanting to lose weight can be a real desire, but setting the goal and sticking to it are sort of abstract concepts for our brain, while all the things that distract us are very well-understood by it. Think about all the points I've already made, and then take a look at your fat-loss goal. You're trying to abstain from doing things, like eating flavorful foods that are bad for you, in order to achieve something nebulous that lies weeks in your future at the very least. The survival of your species has been dependent on immediate gratification throughout its entire history, but you're asking for something foreign.

Your body's goals: consume, rest, be happy right now.

Fat-loss goals: abstain, move, wait a long time for results.

It's no wonder that so many people struggle with fat-loss goals more than any other type of goal. The odds are stacked against us from the ground up. Some of the biggest obstacles in your path are written into your genetic code.

I'm not telling you any of this to depress you, but to help you understand what you are. You can do whatever you want with your body. If you want to be lean and healthy, you can do that, but you probably can't do it in any sustainable way if you don't even understand your own animal behavior. You're not going to sidestep these survival traits just because you really want to wear smaller pants. These things are part of the baked-in goodness that makes you a human. You'll need to work *with* these things, not against them. When long-term goals are a foreign concept, you can't depend on them to be your driving force. Change must happen in other ways. Don't worry, we'll get to that.

Chapter Three
The Hedonic Treadmill and
Why You Can't Get There from Here

NOW THAT YOU have a little better understanding of what you are, and hopefully a little more compassion for your body, let's talk about expectations. I find that most people approach fat-loss goals from a purely emotional place, and it can be really helpful to take a look at the outcomes of those goals from a rational vantage point.

There's a good chance you've told yourself, "I'll be happy when I'm thin." Maybe you don't use those exact words, but something similar is likely going on in your head. You see yourself in a mirror or in a photo, and you very much want to see a different you.

Now for the million-dollar questions: Why? Why do you want to change the way your body looks? What do you think is going to happen?

Simply posing these questions has gotten me in some real trouble. Sometimes I'm hit with heated responses like, "What kind of stupid question is that? I'll be happier, of course!"

Really? What happened all the other times you've said that in your life? You've certainly made other such claims. "I'll be happy when _____ happens." We've all said it.

"When I finally get that job/raise/car/house/relationship, I will be so happy!"

So did it work? When you got that raise you'd been hoping for, and you were suddenly making substantially more money, were you delivered unto the land of bliss? Did you float on air from then on, living the life of a fairy princess, surrounded by rainbows and unicorns? Of course not. You were elated for a while, and then you settled into a new normal. If you were generally unhappy before, you were generally unhappy after. A pay raise can relieve stress about money, but if you're an unhappy person, then you'll always find something else upon which you can blame your unhappiness.

There's a term in psychology called the "hedonic treadmill," and it describes what's happening here. We tend to pursue things and events as if they will somehow *make* us happy, when in reality true happiness is not something you find in external stimuli; it's something you find in yourself. Getting a new car can be really exciting and emotional, but emotions always fade. Happiness is more a state of being than an emotion.

You've been wrong every time you've told yourself that you'd be happy when you finally got or achieved something, so why should fat loss be any different? I find it interesting that out of all the things and events a person might chase in her pursuit of happiness, fat loss is the easiest for us to exclude from the rules of the hedonic treadmill. In my example above, I'm sure it was easy to make you see that a raise does not impart true happiness, but even now you might be fighting this idea when you think about your body. "Damn, Jason," you say. "I've been miserable in this body for so long that I just can't get behind what you're proposing here. Finally looking the way I want to look will definitely make me happier."

Let's return to my original questions. What do you think is going to happen when you like the way your body looks? (Please note that I said, "When *you* like the way your body looks." We're coming back to that later.) Will the world treat you differently? Will someone kick in your door, throw large amounts of money at you, and force you to date movie stars? No, those things won't happen. In fact, a few people complimenting you on your weight loss as they pass you in the hall at work is about the most miraculous thing you can expect.

What do you see in your friends and acquaintances? Do you know many people who have finally reached their fat-loss goals and then achieved some new level of happiness that permeates their lives? Probably not. You might know people who've lost weight and kept it off, and those people might smile with pride when you mention it, but I imagine they're still the same people underneath. If they were unhappy before, then they still are.

What about the people you know who've always had attractive bodies? They're totally happy all the time, right? Sorry, no. Some may be happy, but most probably don't seem to have any idea that they already have what you want. They likely go through their lives just like everybody else, looking for something that they think they need in order to be happy, but happiness will never work that way.

"Well, I'll at least be more confident," you exclaim. I don't really believe that, but let's examine it anyway. If you're not confident now, and the sole reason that you lack confidence is because you don't feel comfortable with the shape of your body, then you are making a choice to be unconfident. We can easily find proof of this in the world around us. I have no doubt that you know someone—or multiple someones—who is bigger than you or otherwise less physically attractive than you, yet she carries herself like she loves and respects everything she is. We all know people like that. There's no line in the sand beyond which everyone becomes insecure. We don't, for example, all lose our confidence at exactly 30 pounds of extra body fat. Since confidence is subjective and not directly correlated to body shape, your current lack of confidence is a choice.

We can say the same for every other character trait that you might be trying to blame on the shape of your body. You could be more gregarious, outgoing, assertive, and generally happy right now, without losing a pound, and the evidence is all around you. I'm not saying that you can just throw a switch and turn these things on, but there's no need to pretend that you can have them only if you lose weight. In fact, you likely have the cart before the horse.

Chapter Four
The Aesthetic Goal Conundrum

IT HAS BECOME apparent to me that people with fat-loss goals generally fall into two categories. I'm generalizing here, and there are varying degrees within these categories, but please play along.

The first group comprises approximately nine out of ten people who come to me. When I ask them why they want my help, they tell me that they want to lose weight. Then, when I press them for details, the message I get is one of poor body image, frustration, and often desperation. In the most extreme examples, some women will even pinch and poke various parts of their bodies to illustrate their disgust. The underlying tone of the exchange is, "I don't like this body. It betrayed me. Can you please tell me how to escape it or force it to comply with my desires? I just can't take this anymore."

Unfortunately, these people almost always struggle and usually fail to reach their goals. They need fast results to stay motivated, they're constantly weighing themselves, they're always on the verge of jumping ship in favor of the next trick or gimmick, and they're largely incapable of seeing any of the other health benefits that might indicate that they're still on their way to achieving their goals—despite the fact that the scale didn't budge this week. Without a major perspective shift, they're just passing through.

The remaining group, the one in ten people, have a point of view that might not seem dramatically different but is in fact a massive advantage. When I ask about their motivations, their response sounds something like, "You know, I'm not really sure when it happened, but I've sort of let myself go, and I'm not okay with that. It's time for me to take better care of myself. I deserve better than this."

With this healthy perspective, these people almost always get amazing results. Since they don't have any desperation in their motives, they just do what needs to be done and enjoy the process. They're not jumping on the scale to see if it's "working" after every tiny effort they make, because doing what they know they need to do *is* the goal. They don't have any fanciful notions about how much more they'll be loved when they finally lose weight, and they see the aesthetic changes in their bodies as icing on the cake.

More than a few times I've heard complaints from these people regarding their fat loss and the folks in the other camp. They say, "I feel fantastic, I sleep great, my sex drive is back, I have tons of energy, I can actually play with my kids (or grandkids) on the playground instead of just watching, and I'm enjoying hobbies that I had given up because I didn't feel good. But all these people want to talk about is how much weight I've lost. I appreciate the compliment, but it seems so shallow compared with everything else I've gained."

When I said at the end of the last chapter that you might have the cart before the horse, this is what I was getting at. Assuming that losing weight will make you feel good about yourself is probably a bad idea, and we'll dig into that more in a moment, but losing weight *because* you feel good about yourself certainly seems to make things a lot easier.

To sum up these thoughts, my vast anecdotal experience has shown that a happy woman will have an easier time reaching her health and fat-loss goals, and the new vitality she gains along the way may *add* to her happiness by allowing her to experience more of a life she already enjoys. On the other hand, a woman who is unhappy because she doesn't like the way she looks won't find happiness in a change of appearance, if she can even get there, but more often than not, she'll be the biggest obstacle in her own path, sabotaging herself in a multitude of ways. Yo-yo dieting, angst, and frustration are the norm on that path.

Chapter Five
Extrinsic vs. Intrinsic Motivations

THE DIFFERENCE BETWEEN our two types of people in the aesthetic goal conundrum lies in their motivations. The more populous group—the ones who typically struggle—are extrinsically motivated. They would be doing none of this on a desert island without other people around to judge them. They change the way they eat and exercise only in an attempt to garner the love and approval of others, and "others" usually means strangers and acquaintances. Their friends and family already love them, so all the desperate madness they put themselves through is for people who probably shouldn't really matter. But, alas, this is the truth of it.

Extrinsic motivations equate to a distaste for the process. When you're only working out to appeal to other people, every trip to the gym is forced and every exercise is a chore. When you're only making healthy food choices because you want to be liked, every bite is another unsatisfying moment when you could be eating foods that make you "happy." The temptation to quit will always be lurking in the shadows, waiting for the right moment to overwhelm you and send you to the couch with a carton of ice cream and a mixing spoon.

The exact opposite of this can be found in the intrinsically motivated person. This is a person who loves the process and loves every amazing benefit that it bestows upon her, no matter how small. Exercising is a joy because it leaves her feeling fantastic, physically and psychologically. It's the same for her food choices. She doesn't miss pizza because she doesn't miss feeling bloated and tired. She isn't tempted to deviate from her plan because she enjoys all of it.

If the intrinsically motivated woman were trapped on a desert island, she would eventually find a way to do some responsible exercise. She doesn't need you or me around to tell her that those squats make her butt look good. She also won't end up doing squats until she can barely stand on her own two feet, because exercise is not a way that she proves anything to anyone. It's all about her and nobody else. The fact that you *do* think her butt looks great is just a nice little side benefit. She appreciates your compliment, but it doesn't motivate her.

Where do you find yourself? If proper diet and exercise feel like a cross for you to bear, then you're probably not ready for change. You need to be able to look at yourself in the mirror and truthfully say that you deserve to be healthy and fit. You have to be able to follow through, and that won't be easy unless you can find some modicum of joy in the small steps. What's the point of forcing yourself through choices that make you miserable just to pursue long-term benefits that are so nebulous and small? Call a spade a spade and return to working on your mind-set until you reach a time when you might actually stand a chance of succeeding.

Chapter Six
You Can't Fix a Body You Hate

IT'S A COMMON thing in the weight-loss industry to encounter people who believe they can go from hating their bodies to loving them just by making themselves smaller. In my experience, this just isn't true.

If you are someone whose inner voice slings insults at you while you brush your teeth in front of the mirror every morning, then when you lose weight, you will simply whip out a magnifying glass and step closer to the mirror so that you can continue your body loathing on a more detailed level. Self-loathing is not solved by changing the way a body looks.

If someone does happen to lose weight and appear more outgoing and confident, then she is inevitably displaying shallow representations of these traits. She looks in the mirror and thinks (maybe subconsciously), "I'm pretty sure I look a little better, and Mary said I look like I lost weight, so I'm going to go out into the world and see who else will give me the approval I need to feel good about myself." The compliments she receives are like a drug, but they don't last, and since approval is so desirable to her, she feels bad when the compliments quit coming. Without approval, she returns to her old assumptions that when she finally gets her body to look just right, then she'll be happy.

This isn't confidence, and it's certainly not happiness. Confidence doesn't require affirmation or approval. On the contrary, confidence is completely oblivious. It simply drives you to do things—not to do things and then look around to see who likes what you did.

What I'm actually saying here is that you *can* hate your body and change the way it looks, but it's highly unlikely that changing the way your body looks will make you quit hating it. When you don't stop hating it, you won't stop trying to change it. Eventually you will break your metabolism and go back to the starting line, where you'll talk about how great you used to look, never mentioning that you hated your body then, too.

Gyms across the world at this very moment are replete with examples of people who have no idea that they've already made it to the finish line. They power through insane workouts and ridiculous diet regimens because they can't seem to turn off their self-criticism, despite the fact that so very many people would do almost anything to look like them. Don't get me wrong; there are plenty of truly healthy people in those gyms, too, but the desperate types stick out like a sore thumb if you look with honest eyes.

It's my hope that you're starting to see the futility in this endless, unwinnable battle. If you are, then I'm sure you're beginning to wonder what you can do about it. We'll get to that, but please understand that you need to know these facts at least as much as you need to know how to fix them, and maybe more. Every epiphany you come to is another pillar that will support your future efforts to become better and stronger.

Chapter Seven
Examining Body Image—an Exercise

JENNY, WHOM WE met in the introduction, showed us one way that a woman might find herself in a body she doesn't like, but there are many other ways to get there. Your own journey has been unique, and the outcome has probably had similar results, but with different painful memories and the resulting aversions and blind spots that they impart. If, for example, you were in a relationship in which someone told you that you were fat every day, then you probably don't take compliments well, and you might not trust yourself when it comes to picking a new partner, because you aren't confident that you'll see the red flags that you should have seen in your old relationship.

I've seen how powerful and freeing it can be when a woman examines her own body image closely. A couple of years ago, I was helping a client try to come to some solid conclusions about how she got to where she was in her head, and the surprising end result for me was that we inadvertently created a very useful exercise.

I truly hope that you'll follow the rules exactly as I lay them out, because this won't work any other way. I'm not promising anything life-altering, but I'm not ruling it out, either. This will be a cognitive approach to helping you find a way to view your body and your thoughts differently. The information you gather about yourself here will be very useful going forward. I know most people will just read through this section without actually doing what I ask, but don't be most people. I've used this exercise with many people so far, and everyone has found it helpful, some going as far as to say they will forever have a healthier point of view. Maybe that could be you. Why not give it a shot?

Okay, here we go:

<u>Step 1</u>

I'd like you to sit down someplace where you can really think and write out the entire story of your poor body image. This should be a detailed history of every single thing that got you to the point where you are now. From the very first time you realized that the way you look matters to other people, to every insult you ever received from any rotten kid in school, to every comment ever made by a friend or loved one. Include absolutely *everything*. If it's helpful, you can use Jenny's story as an example. It's important that you don't leave anything out, and you should write as if nobody but you will ever read it, because nobody has to. Write *your* body image story to *you* in the same voice you use to talk to yourself.

I know I'm asking a lot of you. This is probably going to hurt a little, maybe a lot. Some of the things you write down will be the same things you try hard to never think about. I can't make any of those things go away, but trust me: I have a plan. When we're done, it's my hope that you'll have a new perspective, or at least a clear path to one.

STOP RIGHT HERE! If you read further without completing the above task, you'll render this exercise useless. It absolutely will not work if you know what's coming. To read beyond this point is to commit to not doing this exercise. You have been warned.

Step 2

How did it go? You probably reviewed some painful stuff. Maybe you even had to stop and walk away from the exercise for a while. There's a good chance you even cursed my name a few times for asking you to do this. I know, I understand, and I'm sorry. I wouldn't have asked this of you if I didn't think some deep inspection would help. There is a method to my madness.

Let's get to the point. I want you to go back through your list of events and tally up the facts.

"What? It's all fact! It all happened to me!"

I hear you, and I know it seems that way, but let's look really closely.

If some rotten kid in seventh grade told you that you were fat, that event could be listed as a fact because it actually happened, and you didn't infer anything.

However, if you watched all the popular boys ask girls who were thinner than you to go to prom with them, you cannot say that they didn't ask you to prom because you were fat. There are plenty of reasons to not ask someone to prom other than the size of her body. If, for example, you were already convinced that you were ugly by this point in your life, then there's a damn good chance that you made yourself unapproachable (we're coming back to this soon).

"But I *was* fat," You say. "I was a size 14!" Okay, there actually were thinner girls than you, but that's not the question at hand. The question is whether the boys didn't ask you out *because* you were fat. If you have definitive proof of this, then mark it down as a fact, but definitive proof would have to be completely free of any assumptions. Basically, a boy would have had to say, "No, I won't go out with you because you're fat." Unless something along these lines was said, you have no proof. If it was said, then mark it as a fact.

Here's another example. A guy walked past you, looked you over from head to toe, gave you a disgusted look, and walked away. If something like this made your list, then you will need to acknowledge that a lot must be inferred here if you're using this situation to confirm your negative body image. What if you reminded him of a person who broke his heart? What if you had just cut him off in traffic, never seeing him, but he thought you were being a jerk on purpose? What if he mistook you for someone else who really did deserve his scorn? Between the two of us, we could invent these scenarios all day, couldn't we? In reality, you can't read his mind, and he didn't tell you what he was thinking.

Hopefully you get my point now. Go back over your written history and mark the entries that are purely factual—nothing inferred, nothing assumed, no input from your inner voice—and make a separate list of all the facts. Here are some examples of facts that I've seen when helping people with this exercise:

- Mom did Weight Watchers my whole life, and she taught me to hate my body the way she hated hers.
- My dad called my mom fat in front of me.
- A boyfriend left me after I gained weight, and he actually told me that he was leaving because of my weight gain.

These are factual statements. I know I'm beating this thing to death, but your list of facts cannot include anything that isn't as clear as these examples. When your list is complete, take a new look. I won't try to downplay anything you went through, and some of the possibilities are certainly horrible, but the first purpose of this exercise is to realize that you likely have a lot fewer valid reasons to feel the way you do than you originally thought. If you used some of these solid facts to jump to lots of other conclusions, then it might feel like you've lived a lifetime of confirmation after confirmation that everyone is judging you for your weight. It's more likely that a handful of incidents have helped *you* to practice jumping to the same conclusion over and over again.

My hope is that looking at a small list of facts, as opposed to a lengthy essay littered with emotions and assumptions, will be freeing for you. Your list might still contain some real doozies, but if you're anything like the people I've done this exercise with, the total volume of incidents behind your body image issues should be dramatically reduced.

If I hit my mark, you can now say, "This doesn't really seem like enough reasons for me to hate my body so much." There's more to this exercise, and more very important examination coming up, but if you feel like some introspection is in order, then maybe this is a good place to put this book down and think about what we've been discussing thus far.

Step 3

We have a bit more to learn if we want to get the most out of this exercise. There's still some reframing to do before the real work of changing forever can begin. Now it's time to analyze your list of facts with the most rational parts of your adult brain and without the most emotional parts.

If your dad told you every day of your childhood that you were fat, what does your rational adult brain tell you about him now? Does it tell you that Dad was a wonderful, well-balanced, compassionate, good person whose opinions should be held in high regard? Probably not. Your rational brain might not tell you to hate your father, and you may love him very much, but his behavior in those moments is something for which you should pity him. Those hurtful words were an example of his shortcomings, not a display of his wisdom and good character.

From a different angle, let's say I told you that *my* father told *me* I was fat and ugly my whole life. What would you think of him? Not awesome, right? You wouldn't say to yourself, "I need to meet this guy! He sounds amazing!" All right, then why let *anyone* who acted less than awesome change your perspective? Why is one man (your father) correct and the other (my father) just a jerk? Why listen intently to the words of one but see only the poor character of the other?

When you examine your list, it should be the same for each fact—just bad people being bad (or maybe fairly decent people temporarily making bad decisions, but the outcome is roughly the same). Three times now I have heard of doctors playing the jerk role. One client told me that a doctor told her mother to put her on a diet when she was a kid because it was the only thing that would fix her knee pain. This was his advice for (and in front of) a child who was not small, but was by no means fat. This man doesn't deserve a seat on anyone's Body Image Council! He's terrible at his job and worse at communicating. People like this should be deemed unworthy and left behind, not held in high regard, which is what you're doing when you use such a person's opinion to establish your worth.

But the damage is done. I get it. Reframing the source of the problem is a start, but it isn't a miracle cure for poor body image. You're still going to walk into new situations with people you don't know and promptly jump to the conclusion that they all think you're fat. Why? Because this is the response that you've been *practicing* for years. The only way to change this response will be to practice a new one.

What about all those other entries on your list, the ones that turned out to be less factual and more emotional? They're proof that input from your inner voice is required when you jump to conclusions about what everyone else thinks of you. Very few people in total, and virtually none of them worth your undying respect, are telling you the things you tell yourself. You don't have enough solid facts from your past to make these assumptions. Sure, you can look in the mirror and say that *you* think you're fat, but you can't impose those opinions on the rest of us, and we haven't told you a damn thing.

In effect, nearly all your suffering has been at your own hands. But if you don't consciously and purposefully change your mental habits, you will be this self-abusive person forever. Bad things don't stop happening just because you know about them.

Change requires work. You won't become something better by sitting around hoping for it or allowing yourself to believe you are a victim without any control over your situation. Try to approach changing the health of your thoughts like you would approach changing the health of your body.

Too many women know full well that their motivations for fat loss are wrong and that their personal psychology regarding body image is unhealthy, yet they aren't doing anything to work on those things. The assumption is that they can't do anything to fix their heads, so they put all their energy into the next diet or workout protocol, praying to the gods of fitness and fat loss that this one will finally be the miracle they've been looking for. There's no need for this nonsense. You absolutely can change. No, it won't be easy, but it can be done. I'll show you how before we're done here, but right now we have to keep digging.

Chapter Eight
The Result of Poor Body Image

REGARDLESS OF WHETHER or not you have a valid reason to believe it—and I have just demonstrated that you probably don't—bad things tend to happen when you decide you're unattractive. Everyone else on earth could think that you're fat and ugly, and the result of all those negative opinions will never affect you nearly as much as the moment when you decide that you agree with them.

Remember those people we talked about earlier who are bigger than you yet appear totally confident and happy? Sometimes they've made a choice to be the way they are, and sometimes they're just unaware that anything might not be great about them. Either way, the opinions of others are irrelevant to these confident individuals. They're secure and happy because they don't believe they have reason not to be.

Once you start looking for reasons to feel bad about yourself, you *will* find them, and you will own those (mostly manufactured) reasons and become what you *believe* you are instead of what you actually are. Yes, I know this sounds like something you might hear from a guru on a mountaintop, but it's true. You present yourself to the world as the person you believe you are, thereby becoming what your inner voice has molded you into.

Let's return for a moment to the example I used earlier of the young woman who assumed that the reason she didn't get asked to prom was because she was overweight. She saw the boys asking thinner girls to prom, so she jumped to a conclusion that seemed rational at the time. Let's make the not-so-far-fetched assumption that this young woman has held the belief that she's fat and unattractive since shortly after puberty. By the time prom rolls around, her behavior has been altered by her belief. She's gotten good at blending into the background because she's convinced that each interaction with someone new is a new risk of repeating one of the painful experiences that started her on this path to begin with. Someone said some horrible things to her in the past, and now she protects herself by being unapproachable.

When she does try to be more outgoing, everyone can sense how hard she's trying and how terrified she really is. The people around her respond predictably by not getting too invested in her because they can't possibly understand why she's always either hiding or awkward. She takes this as more proof of her belief about herself. "See, they don't want to like me! It's because I'm fat and ugly!"

Her belief is reflected in her posture as she slumps her shoulders and keeps her head down. It's reflected in the wary look on her face, her lack of eye contact, and the timid half-smile she gives anyone who addresses her. She's hoping she'll only ever be noticed on her own terms—on those rare occasions when she's feeling brave enough to take a halfhearted chance at interacting with people outside her trusted circle of friends. When she's called into the spotlight against her will, she doesn't have enough time to don her "I'm cool" mask. The result is transparency, and her insecurities show through.

Does it sound like I'm describing a fun prom date? No, it doesn't. Our young friend sounds unhappy and hard to talk to. She sounds guarded and reserved. She sounds like she might even try too hard and embarrass herself. But what part of all this is related to the shape of her body? Not one tiny sliver of it! Everything we're talking about in this example is about what she *believes* she is, not what she actually is. Again, she already knows at least a few people who look similar to her but have none of the same beliefs. Those people will be at prom. She has bought into the unsubstantiated (or very weakly substantiated) garbage that her nasty little inner voice is selling to her, and she has personified her belief by becoming unattractive through her actions and mannerisms.

Since life is rarely fair, there are insecure idiots out there who see her weakness and use it against her to make themselves feel better. These are the bullies who actually do make things worse for her by saying terrible things that nobody worthwhile would ever say. They don't make these attacks because she's unattractive, but because they can tell that *she thinks* she's unattractive. Her worst fear is realized *because of* her worst fear. It's a brutal positive feedback loop.

Through it all, this young woman will set her mind to "fixing" this problem by trying to change the way she looks. She will bring all her desperation and anxiety into her painful and frustrating fight against the wrong problem. We've already been over why she is almost certain to fail.

Chapter Nine
Attraction

I FIND THE topic of attraction in humans to be extremely fascinating. However, it's a subject that seems to be largely misunderstood, primarily because we simply respond to natural cues and emotions without ever analyzing what's really behind them. The resultant misunderstanding is particularly hard on women in modern society.

(A quick disclaimer: this section is written predominantly to heterosexual women, although I think most of the same rules probably apply to non-heterosexual attraction. This is not because I'm trying to be insensitive to other sexual preferences, only that this entire book is written from my own experience, and I haven't worked with many LGBT people. To be honest, I have no idea why that's been the case, and I have always sincerely hoped that it's a numbers issue and not a "me" issue.)

It seems to me that most women are getting their definition of beauty from the media, but it's important to note that the media is trying to sell you things, and it can best accomplish its goals by making you insecure. Interestingly, you've never dated the media. Romantic relationships happen between real individuals, and the examples being set before you every single day of your life do not support what the media tells you, yet you probably ignore the truth in front of you and believe the media instead. What I mean is that you can see real couples in the real world. Are all the good men married only to women who resemble what the media tells you is perfect? Of course not! Happy couples come in all aesthetic flavors.

It's easy to fall into the trap of believing that your body must be "perfect," but plus-sized models are an affront to that belief. When I've asked big groups of women what they think of a particular plus-sized model like Ashley Graham (the first plus-sized model to appear on the cover of Sports Illustrated's Swimsuit Issue), they tell me things like, "She's pretty, but that's not what the media tells us we should look like." Interestingly, virtually all honest men will say she's gorgeous.

However, if someone were to post a picture of Ashley Graham in a high-traffic online venue and ask men to rate her, there would certainly be hundreds, maybe thousands, of horrible comments posted, and women onlookers would yell, "See? She's not thin enough! This proves it!" That conclusion seems to make sense, but it's wrong.

Those men who say terrible things will be almost exclusively young jerks who aren't really commenting on Ashley's body. They could be trying to take a jab at women in general because making women feel insecure is the only way they can get anyone to date them, but usually their motives aren't about women at all. What's really happening there is much more about rank. If some young punk says, "No way, she's fat," what he's actually saying is, "All you other men said she was beautiful, but not me. I said she wasn't beautiful, so clearly I can do better than her and you are all beneath me. I'm the winner!" Unfortunately, women won't see it for the power play that it is, which makes sense because even the young punks probably don't truly understand their actions. Instead, women will use the fake opinions of these idiots to affirm what they believe they knew all along.

The basic difference between the genders when it comes to attraction (and I'm generalizing here) is that women typically *attract* mates, while men can *earn* them. A man can outrank his competition and be deemed more attractive by earning more money, accumulating more power, and sometimes even through a better physical display, like athletic ability. He can also be funnier, more artistic, or more intelligent than his peers and win the affections of the woman he pursues. All these things are indications that he is capable of providing for their offspring, but that's not how she will see it on the surface. Women don't usually look at a handsome, accomplished man who carries himself well and think, "He would be a good father to my children." However, the emotions she does feel were evolved to suit that exact purpose.

Disney movies and romance novels have led us all to believe that something more magical is going on, but in reality attraction is about the propagation of our species. We can tell ourselves whatever we like, and we each make our own decisions about whether or not we want to breed, but none of this changes the fact that there is such a thing as human attraction only because nature wants us to make babies. Therefore, an individual's attractiveness is about the display of his or her genetics. Physically, we're attracted to displays of health. We'll be coming back to that subject, but for now let's focus on the fact that physical attraction is just a small part of the whole of attraction in humans.

I'm not a zoologist, but physical attraction might be nearly everything in the tiger mating game. Alas, we are not tigers. We are weak, hairless apes. We have no claws or sharp teeth. Our bodies, aside from our opposable thumbs, have had only a small effect on our outrageous success as a species when compared with our great big brains. It was our cunning, intelligence, and ingenuity that allowed us to survive, so it's impossible to separate our brains from our bodies when it comes to attraction. In short, the human mind functions very well as a sexual display.

Evolutionary psychologist Geoffrey Miller paints a beautiful picture in his amazing book *The Mating Mind* of just how "the human mind and the peacock tail may serve similar biological functions." He says, "The human mind's most impressive abilities are like the peacock's tail: they are courtship tools, evolved to attract and entertain sexual partners." Miller tells us that our brains offer a host of new "fitness indicators," or displays of good genetics, to potential mates. Or, in his words, "The healthy brain theory proposes that our minds are clusters of fitness indicators: persuasive salesmen like art, music, and humor, that do their best work in courtship where the most important deals are made." He goes on to say, "Most evolutionary psychologists agree that human mate choice is even more focused on mind than on body, concerned as it is with assessing a person's social status, intelligence, kindness, reliability, and other psychological traits."

From my male perspective, this is the first thing that so many women seem to misunderstand when they fixate on physical attraction at the expense of their other traits. When a woman with a "perfect" body lacks confidence, charisma, vitality, and true happiness, she will absolutely still attract men, but not in the way that she wishes she would. This brings me to my next point.

Returning to the unromantic subject of our biology, we see that women have a much greater commitment to procreation than do men. It's the woman's body that grows the fetus and feeds the baby from conception through the first couple of years, but even prior to that the woman supplies the greater contribution to conception. Eggs are in short supply when compared with sperm, which are manufactured in the tens of millions, and eggs are a much more complicated cell to begin with.

This biology explains why female attraction to males is more complex than male attraction to females: Females must be far choosier to be successful. This is evident in the fact that magazines like Playgirl have never sold to women with anywhere near the success that Playboy has sold to men. A woman needs to see the way a man carries himself and needs some information regarding the kind of man he is before she can become truly attracted to him on a deep level. Since her commitment to childbirth and child rearing is so high, she might be capable of hooting and hollering at the occasional male strip show in Las Vegas, but she is not looking for a mate there.

Now for the other concept that women typically seem to overlook, much to their own detriment. Evolutionary biologist and bestselling author Richard Dawkins has said, and I'm paraphrasing here, that no male mammal ever has a strong reason to turn down an opportunity to copulate with any female. With a lower contribution to making babies, most male mammals' primary concern will be to spread their genetics as far and wide as possible. It's a quantity-over-quality thing.

Human males are more prone to monogamy than most mammals, but attraction in us still works a bit differently than it does in women. For men, sexual attraction and long-term relationship attraction can be separate subjects. Back to our Playboy example, men can be sexually attracted to the mere silhouette of a female body without knowing anything about the woman at all. Sadly, some frustrated women will focus on this one piece of information and assume they "get" what men want, calling us pigs and then focusing almost exclusively on their own physical appearance when they try to increase their attractiveness. What is overlooked is the often vast difference between sexual attraction and what you are hoping we really see in you.

Here's an example. Pick the top female train-wreck celebrity of the moment. You know the one: She's pretty, she's rich, she's everywhere, and the tabloids love to talk about her exploits in nightclubs and elite parties. I'm going to do the smart thing and refrain from naming names, but I'm sure you have someone in your head. Now ask a trusted man in your life to poll his friends for you by asking them the following two questions (you can't ask them yourself because, since you're a woman, most men won't be truthful with you):

1. If you are/were single, would you sleep with (insert train-wreck celebrity woman), no strings attached?
2. If you are/were single, would you enter into a long-term relationship with (insert train-wreck celebrity woman)?

If the majority of the men polled by your trusted male friend were older than 25 and not influenced by something like a religious ideology that prohibits sex outside of marriage, I can guarantee that they answered yes to question 1 and some version of "Hell, no!" to question 2.

You are going to have to get around the anger and distaste that you might be feeling after what you've just read. Men are not attracted to women in the exact same way that women are attracted to men, and this fact makes perfect sense when you eliminate emotions and look at attraction through the lens of evolutionary biology. Despite the fact that so many women use this information as a reason to be frustrated with men, it can and should be used to set you free.

When you walk into a party and see a group of guys vying for the attention of a beautiful blonde, you can be assured that these men are not trying to figure out a way to make her fall in love with them. Okay, that might not be entirely fair, because she could very well be an amazing person, but that's not what you're focusing on, and you know it. You are looking at her and the attention she is getting, comparing her aesthetic appeal to your own, and then feeling bad about yourself. I'm proposing that you would not feel that way if you could be one of those men for a day.

I'm going to go out on a limb and assume that you probably want to be loved and appreciated for everything you are. You want a man to treat you like you are his everything. You don't want to be treated like a body to be used for nothing more than the short-term appeasing of animal instincts. So why do you look at those animal displays and think they say something about your own overall attractiveness? Yes, that woman might have an advantage over you when it comes to making men want to sleep with her, but you want much more than that! Regardless of what you might have reduced us to, men don't marry bodies. We engage in long-term relationships with the most wonderful *whole* woman we can find and convince to lower her standards enough to give us a shot. Do you honestly believe that good bodies make great women?

"Dammit, Jason, I am a wonderful person with lots of amazing qualities, but men never give me a chance because I'm not as pretty as some of the other women! It takes good looks to get their attention in the first place!"

I hear you, but we've been over this. You present to the world the person you believe you are. There are no hard, impassible lines out there. Lots of women whom you might judge to be unattractive were deemed sexy as hell by their wonderful husbands. You've seen this many times in those couples who made you think, "How did she get him?" She got him by thinking better of herself than you do.

I just want you to try to imagine that attraction might not be exactly what you think it is. While it's an unfortunate fact of our evolution that women and men differ in some of our innate animal drives, if you don't always overlay your own thoughts and ideals onto the world around you, you can be free to be the awesome person you really are instead of trying so hard to be nothing more than the physical body you think you should be.

Chapter Ten
What Every Woman Needs to Know About Men and Testosterone

I HAVE ONE more quick point to make regarding attraction, this time for the women in long-term relationships with men. There's a sad scenario that I've seen played out too many times, and it comes down to nothing more than an unfortunate misunderstanding. Let's use Jenny as an example again.

Jenny has been fed a lot of bad advice over the years, and she has body fat that she would very much like to lose. Even though Jenny's doctor says she is "healthy," what he really means is "not sick," and since bodies in peak health always look great, we know that Jenny is not in peak health. In her female body, subpar health manifests itself in erratic periods, moodiness, a slow thyroid, low energy, and weight gain.

Scott, Jenny's husband, lives the same lifestyle as Jenny. They eat the same foods, move their bodies in similar ways each day, keep roughly the same sleep schedule, and deal with many of the same stressors. Scott has low energy and moodiness, but aside from a little belly squishiness, he never puts on much fat.

However, the same lifestyle choices that made Jenny gain weight cause Scott's testosterone to drop. When his testosterone drops, so does his sex drive. With a much-reduced sex drive, Scott only rarely initiates sex these days, and usually only when he's been drinking alcohol. Jenny has no clue that the lifestyle they both lead is the real cause of Scott's lack of sex drive, but she does know that she despises the way she looks, so she's certain that Scott is no longer turned on by her because she's overweight. This "fact" in her mind only serves to increase her desperation and anxiety.

Scott, unfortunately, has no idea what is going on. His drop in testosterone and subsequent loss of sex drive are subtle, mostly subconscious things. He's not likely to wake up one day and think, "Hey, why don't I want sex like I used to?" If a thought like that does happen to reach his conscious mind, he'll probably chalk it up to aging, especially if he talks to his buddies and finds out that they're all in the same boat.

If Jenny gets frustrated enough, she might ask Scott why he doesn't find her attractive anymore, to which he will reply, "Of course I find you attractive! Don't be silly! You're beautiful and I love you!" But his actions will not tell her what she wants to hear, so she'll continue to believe that her body repels him. She'll do everything in her power to make sure he never gets the slightest glimpse of her when she's naked, and she'll do ever more desperate things to try to lose fat. Unfortunately, all of those things will be aimed at getting smaller, rather than getting healthier. Supportive husband that he is, Scott will generally take the same unhelpful steps, and the problem never goes away.

To sum this up for you, the same things that made you gain weight are likely to have affected the testosterone level of your husband or boyfriend. It's silly to assume that your body is what has ruined your sex life. I'm a man, and you can trust me when I say that no amount of body fat will stop a healthy man from wanting to have sex with the woman he loves, unless that body fat alters the way she carries herself to the degree that she becomes off-putting. Even then, this isn't an issue of the woman's body, but an issue of what she believes. A healthy man could become concerned for the health of the overweight woman he loves, but as long as she's receptive, he will still want sex. It's just part of what it means to be male.

Stop assuming.

Chapter Eleven
Social Comparison and Social Media

PROMINENT POSITIVE PSYCHOLOGIST and my good friend Robert Biswas-Diener has spent some time with the Massai in Africa. The Massai are a people that herd cattle but otherwise live very much like hunter-gatherers. When Robert and his colleagues asked various Massai individuals if they believed themselves to be attractive, the general response was, "Of course I'm attractive." When asked what made them attractive, they usually pointed to adornments like clothing and jewelry instead of features of their own bodies. This is the magic of living in a society where nobody has ever seen her full reflection in a mirror. In order to feel bad about the way you look, you have to know what you look like.

Social comparison is a big part of how we assess ourselves, but comparison on the vast scale that we are capable of today is just another destructive force in the lives of so many women. Not only do you have lots of ways to assess yourself—mirrors, scales, measuring tapes, standard clothing sizes, BMI, machines that measure body fat percentages—you also have an endless supply of other women to compare yourself with. Since you're not perfect, you're absolutely guaranteed to see women on a regular basis who do not have the "flaw" that you have named your biggest insecurity. If you believe you're too short, you'll always notice all the beautiful tall people around you. If you believe you're too tall, those gorgeous shorter women will be everywhere. And, of course, if you believe you're too fat, it won't make any difference that (if you live in the U.S.) 60 percent of the population is overweight. Those damn skinny women will be pouring out of the cracks in the sidewalk.

In my humble opinion, social media has been the worst thing to happen to the psychological well-being and happiness of American women in my 42 years of life. Do you think I'm exaggerating? I'm going to have to do some more generalizing to make my point, but hear me out.

When boys hit puberty, they become concerned with rank. They begin playing sports, talking trash to one another, and sometimes even literally fighting. The less physically competitive boys will usually try to rank at something, too, be it grades, video games, or some sort of collection or expertise. Even nerds talk trash about *something*.

Girls, on the other hand, become concerned with popularity as a way to rank themselves. They are instinctively driven to form social bonds, which some scientists believe might be about banding together to support one another against the knuckle-dragging, mouth-breathing males who didn't always have women's best interests in mind. They will sometimes be called "catty" for their passive-aggressive behavior, but they will vary rarely insult one another as directly as the boys do, because to do so would risk the potential loss of someone who can be counted as a friend—and every name on the list counts.

In short, the most popular boys are popular because of their rank, whereas the highest ranked girls are so ranked because they are popular.

Enter social media. If you're hardwired to be social, supportive, and seek approval from others, sites like Facebook and Instagram act very much like a drug for you. What I mean is that Facebook is to women's social drives what cocaine is to happiness. It's a fake and twisted form of what you naturally seek, but it feels real, even when it's only making you more and more miserable. Let's take another look at Jenny.

Jenny is on Facebook many times a day, usually on her smartphone, which is always at arm's reach. Yesterday, she took six selfies for a new profile photo, but she thought her face looked puffy, and the whole episode nearly ended in tears. Today, she took another nine selfies, and she finally chose one to post. That was three hours ago, and her photo has only seven likes. The last one was twenty-five minutes ago, and she's starting to check Facebook more often now because she's beginning to get her feelings hurt.

Each time Jenny checks her photo, she sees the things her "friends" are posting. She's met very few of these people in real life, but she feels as though she really knows them. Up pops a post from Kelly, a woman she met in a low-carb weight-loss group on Facebook. "Kelly is so pretty," Jenny thinks to herself. "She seems like she has it all—great husband, kids that are good at everything, and she doesn't even have to work! Ugh, I wish I had her life."

What never crosses Jenny's mind is that Kelly is doing exactly what she does. Facebook isn't full of people, it's full of projections of people. It's full of the parts of people that those people want the world to see. While Jenny takes a bunch of pictures before choosing the perfect one, Kelly fails to mention her back pain, her psychotic sister, and her neighbor that makes her whole family miserable every time they go outside.

This is social comparison horribly morphed into something much more destructive by removing the truth and displaying only the shiny bits. Scroll through your social media feed sometime and look at it with fresh eyes. You'll see that each person always seems to be photographed from the same general angle and in the same

couple of poses. When a group of women are photographed together, many will pose in a way so as to hide behind the others or
to obscure their bodies from the camera somehow. In those spur-
of-the-moment pics that can't be edited or thrown out, you'll see a
lot of smiling mouths below terrified eyes.

I understand that social media is highly appealing, but it isn't real.
When you are hardwired to make friends, to be sympathetic, to pat
one another on the back, social media offers you a way to feel like
you're doing that all day long, even when you're actually all alone.
The problem is that it cannot replace real-life human interaction,
which is what you truly crave, but it can and does help you set
unrealistic expectations for yourself by allowing you to compare
yourself with endless fictitious online personas.

Recent research supports my feelings on social media, but I find
my own anecdotal experience to be more powerful. In all my years
of working with women since social media has been a thing, I have
never, *ever* seen a woman substantially reduce social media exposure
without it resulting in a noticeable increase in her happiness.

I implore you: Please consider what I'm saying in this section. You
can be happier in your own skin, but you need to eliminate as much
of the constant social comparison bombardment as you possibly can.
You may think that Facebook is just a way for you to keep in touch
with friends and family that you never see, but then why do you have
so many friends that you either don't know in real life or don't really
care about? Keeping those people around just so you can trade likes
on your posts is not bringing anything of value to your life, but it is
exposing you to more lives to measure yours against.

We may already know too much about ourselves to be like the
Massai, but we can certainly escape the majority of the false
competition. Take control by getting your head back into the real
world. I promise you won't regret it.

Chapter Twelve
A Desire to Be Liked

WE ALL WANT to be liked. It's natural to want to surround ourselves with people who care about us, and most of us achieve this on some level, but sometimes this desire becomes a destructive need. When a need to please others begins to override rational thinking, things can get ugly.

I was talking about this subject with a friend one day, and she gave me an example from her past. She lives in a big city and walks everywhere, so she has no need for a car. One day, she was having a conversation with some of her coworkers, and they were expressing to her that they thought it was strange that she didn't have a car. She told me, "I actually thought about going out and getting a car, even though I totally didn't need one, just because I didn't want these people to think I was odd. I didn't really buy a car, but it's just crazy that the thought crossed my mind."

I have another friend who quit a job that she was good at because the people she worked with didn't seem to like her. Nobody was directly rude to her, but they were very social with one another and never included her in any of their conversations or activities. This one was a shocker for me because my brain doesn't work that way. When I thought about it, I realized that I have probably had jobs in the past where people didn't like me and I had no idea. My male brain was busy focusing on rank, and I never noticed whether or not I was popular.

I'm absolutely not saying that one perspective is better than the other. In fact, it should always feel better to be among people who like you, but is there a high price for you, personally, when it comes to that desire? How much time do you spend worrying about things like a look on someone's face that you can't quite interpret or the tone of an email that is not exactly clear?

At the end of the day, we all have people who truly love us and would never abandon us. Those are the people who could see us make enormous fools of ourselves and say, "Wow, that was rough, but it's over and everything is going to be fine." So when you really think about it, any time spent worrying about being liked is probably just worrying about the opinions of people of very little consequence in our lives.

"Foul!" you cry. "I have to be liked! My success in my job is dependent upon it. And who wants to go through life hated by everyone?"

I understand where these objections are coming from, but I would propose that you have to be *likeable*, not liked. You don't have any control over whether or not someone likes you, and going out of your way to try to get proof that each individual acquaintance in your world thinks you're great is an exhausting endeavor that cannot hope to succeed. That would involve too many factors outside your control.

On the other hand, you absolutely can be likeable. You can behave in a fashion that you know will endear people to you by being kind and treating everyone fairly. You can be compassionate and helpful. You can be witty and thoughtful, making valuable contributions to conversations and tasks. But once you're done offering your awesomeness to the people around you, there's nothing left for you to do. Running around checking to see if it worked, if you're actually liked, is just asking for heartache. The conclusions that other people come to are not up to you.

The magic of this perspective is that it comes from someplace totally inside you. You are being the person you want to be and *deciding* that you're likeable without the need for affirmation. If someone doesn't like you, that is no fault of yours. You've done your part, and you're not interested in figuring out the subtleties of that person's feelings.

This concept applies nicely to fat-loss goals. You can choose your own opinion of your body and leave it at that. "I've got some weight to lose and I'm working on that, but it doesn't change the fact that I'm awesome. Since I'm a good person who does not automatically dislike anyone who doesn't have a perfect body, I will simply assume that the people around me do the same rather than seeking their approval."

Trying to make everyone like you is a great way to spin your wheels and stress yourself out while ruminating on the outcome of your every word, action, and choice. None of this is necessary. The people who love you will love you anyway. Everyone else will probably like you if you like yourself. But in the end, who cares? Just be likeable and call it good.

Chapter Thirteen
Hell Is Other People

I'M SADDENED BY how often I encounter women with loved ones who are unsupportive or who deliberately try to sabotage their fat-loss goals. This is a frustrating subject for me, because all too often I'm unable to help. I'm going to do my best to break down what I have seen and interpreted, and I'll certainly give you my best advice, but I want you to understand up front that I can't help someone who isn't reading this book and isn't trying to improve himself. To say this another way, I can describe the various ways that unsupportive relationships can play out, but when it comes to how to solve the problem, we can only talk about you. It won't do you any good if I help you get angry by pointing fingers and calling names. On the contrary, the only thing that will work is for you to own every part of the situation that you can control. What I'm getting at is that some of this might sting a little. It's not my intent to hurt feelings, but placing blame on others is not the kind of action required for change.

I've seen some very clear correlations throughout my career. These are all generalizations, but they're worth noting. For example, women who have a very strong desire to please others often find themselves in relationships in which they don't have a lot of control once their partners stubbornly plant their feet. Women with low self-worth often find themselves in codependent relationships in which their partners don't really respect them or their desires. And women with low self-confidence usually find themselves in relationships in which their partners don't really believe in them. All of this makes perfect sense from a psychological standpoint. If I were to present my findings to the psychology department at one of my local colleges, I'd be wasting their time. None of this would be news to them.

My point is that I believe any relationship is more likely to be the product of the people in them than the people in them are the product of the relationship. In other words, you may be molded to some degree by your relationships, but what you believe about yourself determines what kind of relationship you end up in to begin with. If you think you suck, you will be more likely to fall for someone because he loves *you*, rather than because you love him. "I don't feel loveable, but he loves me anyway so he's amazing!"

I'm sharing this because you need to understand that the onus is largely on you, even when that really hurts. Outside of one-off situations in which someone is randomly a jerk to you, you are repeatedly treated poorly only because you've decided to allow it. I won't claim to understand your life, and I won't say that there could never be any gray area in these matters, but you're the one holding the reins to your life, and you are *always* making choices.

Okay, back to *them*.

In my experience, unsupportive people come in only a couple of flavors. Since male partners have been the most common saboteurs in my career, we'll start with them.

The biggest problem that I see with many men is just basic, innocent ignorance. Even when men are supportive, they usually have no clue what it's like for you to be a woman and spend so much of your adult life thinking about your body.

When men get out of the shower, even if we are overweight and out of shape, we are far more likely to flex in the mirror than to quickly look away. We could discuss the subtle intricacies of the reasons for this fact, but that would necessitate a lengthy and boring chapter that would travel well outside the scope of this book. Suffice it to say, men are hampered by just as many psychological obstacles in life as women, but those obstacles are very different when it comes to our bodies. For example, you outlive us because we're prone to stressing ourselves into the ground as we compete with one another, but male competition is not about how we look.

When I work with men who have fat-loss goals, the biggest problem we face is almost always compliance. Men very often deviate from the plan I set before them because their motivations don't run deep enough. A male client might know that he "needs to lose weight," but the appearance of his body probably doesn't make him sad or mad. This lack of emotional commitment is usually only overcome in men who either want more muscle (back to the competition thing) or who are driven to truly get healthy. Otherwise, the man who thinks he needs to lose weight in order to be more attractive doesn't say those words to himself with enough conviction to get the job done.

With his radically different perspective, a husband or boyfriend is unlikely to see your years of dieting and frustration as anything that makes sense to him. The angst that you wear on your sleeve in your most vulnerable moments is just not something he can get his head around.

I think it's fair to say that most men will go along for the ride, but the unsupportive men who are left move into two groups: He either doesn't want to be inconvenienced by the changes you're imposing upon him or (much worse) he's insecure and doesn't want you to be better than he is.

In the first group, we have men who don't really dislike their own bodies enough to make major change, but they do like their lives the way they are. If you're doing most of the cooking, a guy in this group will complain and bring home fast food. If he's doing most of the cooking, you don't stand a chance of changing your diet while you're at home.

This situation is made worse by a long history of dieting and desperation on your part. If you've done a lot of crazy diets and exercise plans, he'll probably hold those failed attempts against you, either purposely or subconsciously. Try to remember that none of this makes him a bad person. If he has seen you put yourself through a lot of torture, maybe he just doesn't want you to go through that again. If he doesn't want his own lifestyle altered, then try to understand that he doesn't share your goals.

Communication is the best way to deal with this particular gentleman. You're going to have to sit him down and explain yourself. He needs to hear you tell him that you're working on your head and the relationship you have with your body. He needs you to say, very clearly, that you know you've made a lot of mistakes in the past, but this time is different because you want to try to get healthy instead of just smaller. He needs to hear you actually ask for his support rather than just telling him that you're doing something new (again). He may not agree to change with you, but he just might agree to keeping temptations out of your home.

If you have the other kind of man in your life, the kind who wants you to stay miserable with him, then I'm forced to tell you that the struggles you face with your body are just one more indication of much bigger problems you face with your self-worth. What he gives you is not love; it's codependency. I'm not a relationship counselor, so I won't pretend to have the exact advice you need, but I will say this: In all my life, I've never met a woman who doesn't deserve better than that. This is the only life you get. Please at least consider making better decisions about the people you allow into it.

The unsupportive women in your life usually have an agenda. They either want you to stay like them, or they want you to do what they're doing to lose weight. Both are fairly easy to understand but not always easy to navigate.

Let's be honest: Weight and body image are huge subjects of conversation among women. *Fat talk*, as it has been labeled in recent research, has even been acknowledged as a common form of female bonding. As a man, I'm not privy to the conversations that unfold between women alone, but it's not hard to dig this stuff up. Countless women have said things to me like, "It seems like I never talk to my mom without her mentioning her weight." Or, "When I'm with my friends, the discussion always eventually turns to our bodies and whatever diets we're doing at the time."

When such concerns run so deep as to become an integral part of your relationship with the other women in your life, it makes perfect sense that both you and they would subconsciously create comfort zones around weight and body image. If one woman in the group is improving herself while the others are not ready, then someone is going to end up uncomfortable.

Sadly, I've seen more than a few relationships dramatically altered or even ended when someone I was working with made the decision to get healthy and fit for good. I could do nothing to help. I truly understand both sides of this problem. As a fat-loss coach, I am of course rooting for the success of the women who asked me for help, but I can also easily imagine how it must feel good on some level to gather together with your girlfriends and vent your frustrations in this modern world that so badly wants you to be overweight and unhappy. When the social support you've received from other women for most of your life is at least loosely tied to the camaraderie you feel in these shared frustrations, changing means giving up a lot of soothing reassurance.

It's also worth noting that your friends might not be in a good place in their lives to make the changes you're trying to make, but they might still wish for those changes. In other words, the timing could be wrong for them, and watching you improve yourself might be making them feel bad about their motivation, resolve, confidence, etc. They couldn't follow in your footsteps right now without making things worse for themselves, so they aren't willing to offer you any real support.

The first step with friends and family is the same is it is with unsupportive partners: communication. You're going to have to talk it out. These things don't tend to magically go away. Speak your mind, share your desires, request help, and make decisions based on what you learn. It's okay to say, "I don't need you to understand what I'm doing, but I'm asking for your support."

One last point: You don't need cheerleaders. While it's nice to have someone rooting for you, it's not essential to the process. Plenty of people quietly change their heads, then their habits, and then their bodies while never even talking about those changes with anyone. Maybe keeping your head down will be easier for you than dealing with the naysayers. Of course, that plan also requires the confidence and motivation to follow through without accountability.

I've given you all I have to offer on this touchy subject. I would never suggest that you end any relationships or distance yourself from your friends or family members. Those things will have to be up to you alone. The only suggestion I can make is that you weigh your goals against each of the unsupportive relationships in your life and see where you land. Nobody should ever tell you what your goals should be, and I'm certainly not doing that here. Some analysis is necessary, though. If you try to keep your fat-loss goal at the top of your list of priorities while also surrounding yourself with relationships that don't facilitate that goal, then you will only create a lot of frustration for yourself.

Chapter Fourteen
Self-Sabotage

A NEGATIVE INNER voice can be a destructive force like none other, and nothing has the power to derail you as efficiently as one that says, "You don't deserve success." In my experience, this perspective is extremely common. Even if a person never actually says those exact words to herself, we all have our moments of self-doubt. The results usually play out in one of two ways.

When a self-saboteur finally finds someone like me who stops feeding her tricks and gimmicks and puts her on the path to real long-term success, everything seems magical and wonderful for a while. Then her nasty little inner voice rears its ugly head.

"Why are you torturing yourself?" it asks. "Yeah, you've made some progress, but do you *really* think this is going to work for you? Look at the other people who are getting results. Do you *really* think you're like them? Those people are better than you, and you know it! Stop suffering and eat that damn cheesecake!" How can anyone hold out against such a pernicious argument? It's not like you can walk away from your inner voice.

Not everyone sabotages themselves in this exact way, but all self-sabotage requires negative beliefs and an inner voice that constantly spouts them. Another common perspective is one that says, "I'm a fraud."

When you make positive changes to your health and body, people will eventually notice. This new attention makes some people uncomfortable enough to put everything back the way it was and return to the shadows. Others won't sabotage themselves quite so dramatically, but they will be more vulnerable to temptations because they will constantly question the attention they receive.

Here are a few questions that can help you assess your susceptibility to self-sabotage.

- How do you take compliments? I'm not just asking about how you respond to compliments, but how do they make you feel? If someone tells you that you look nice, do you wonder about the ulterior motives of that person? Do you think, "Clearly I don't look nice, so what does he want from me?"
- When you enter into a new relationship, either with a new romantic partner or a new friend, do you try to hide who you *really* are? "When they discover the real me, this is over. I have to be careful to show them only the *best* me."
- Do you have an online persona that doesn't feel like an accurate representation of your own opinions of yourself? In other words, are you trying to persuade people online to think better of you than you think of yourself?

These questions should be able to tell you how you feel about yourself, but they weren't really necessary, because you probably didn't learn anything new. My point is that self-sabotage is lurking around every corner for people who don't like themselves.

Could you be charitable and kind—all day, every day for weeks, months, and years—to someone you really didn't like? Probably not. You might try, but the fact that you dislike that person will wear on you, because you believe in your heart that she doesn't really deserve your kindness.

Why, then, is it reasonable to believe that you can be kind to yourself if you are also someone you don't like?

This is another mismatch between belief and reality. When you hold the belief that you generally suck, it's easy to jump onboard with fat-loss tricks and gimmicks because they don't require you to love yourself. As usual, you will treat your body like it is the enemy. You're finally going to force it to comply with your wishes by drinking this shake, or taking this supplement, or attending this spin class.

Reality says something different. You're going to have to get really healthy if you want to look great forever, but getting healthy requires treating yourself with love and compassion. As such, when a person who dislikes herself finally finds the path to real health and long-term fat loss success, she will approach that plan like it's just another trick or gimmick. She'll follow the "rules" of that plan without ever understanding the true spirit of what she should be doing—loving the process and feeling great in every moment along the way.

Self-sabotage is a problem of belief. If you are a self-saboteur, you should be able to see a pattern in your past. If the pattern is there, then it doesn't make sense to jump right back into the mix and head straight for the same outcome. Once again, we see that change must start with your head or you should not expect to win.

Chapter Fifteen
Control

I KNOW THIS sounds like one of those ridiculous motivational memes on Instagram, but you can't be successful if you don't fully believe that you can. Ugh. Even typing that felt trite. But there's so much truth to those words.

Psychologists talk about something called "locus of control." It boils down to where you believe the control over your goals lies—within you or in external forces. An internal locus of control is one that says, "I've got this. The task before me may be easy or extremely difficult, but either way I have the ability to complete it." An external locus of control is one that says, "I'll give it a shot, but there are factors involved that I cannot affect. I hope I'll be successful at this task, but I have no guarantees."

The benefit of an internal locus of control is that the concept of "failure" tends to vanish. When you honestly believe you have control over your fat-loss goal, there are opportunities to learn and make adjustments, but there are no failures. This perspective says, "Lots of people get fit and healthy, so of course I can, too. Whenever I come to an impasse, I'll learn more about what I need to achieve my goal."

External loci of control are common in the fat-loss world because they go hand in hand with yo-yo dieting. After trying 10 different tricks to lose weight, you'll likely start to believe that you're part of the problem. The "nothing ever works for me" attitude will infect you like a disease. When you see other people losing weight using techniques that don't work for you, it's understandable to stop believing that you're holding the reins. In reality, those techniques aren't working for most of those other people, either, at least not in the long term, but it doesn't matter once the damage is done to your perspective.

We'll talk in future chapters about what you can do to change your perspective, but it's essential that you understand that an external locus of control is absolutely an obstacle in your path. In order to reach your goals, you have to be actively *doing* things that facilitate those goals as opposed to repeatedly *trying* things that might be the magic you've been looking for. (Seriously, I'm doing my best to not sound like those memes.)

An internal locus of control will allow you to remove emotion from your game and methodically work out the problems before you. An external locus of control will cause you to look for a button that you can push that will finally make everything better. "Carbs! It was carbs all along! My prayers are answered!"

An internal locus of control will allow you to continually add new information to your growing knowledge of how your body works and what it wants to be healthy. An external locus of control throws the baby out with the bathwater with each "failure." "I cut carbs and that didn't work, so now I'm off to the grocery store to buy a cart full of low-fat foods!"

Lifestyle change is hard. We've been over some very real problems we all face along the way to health and sexiness, and we're not done yet. But the belief that you can do it is an essential component of your success. Picture the process of losing fat as if it were an Olympic event. Everyone lines up at the starting line of the big race, and you and your partner each pick your favorite athlete and place a friendly wager. Suddenly, as the runners settle into the starting blocks, you're granted the power to read minds and find that the athlete you chose is thinking, "Woe is me. I'm probably going to lose again. I always lose. I'm terrible at sprinting. I'm sure all these other sprinters are much better than me." How do you feel about that bet now?

As banal as it sounds when someone tells you that you have to believe that you can do something, it's absolutely true. Think about it: Psychologists would not have a term like *locus of control* if it were not a useful thing to understand. What you believe really does affect the outcome of your endeavors.

Here's another example. The gold standard for pharmaceutical drug trials is the double-blind placebo-controlled human clinical trial. The way it works is that some subjects are given the actual drug while others are given a placebo (like a sugar pill), and neither the researchers nor the subjects know what is given to whom. The reason for the *double-blind* part is that if the subjects, the researchers, or both know who gets the real drug and who gets the placebo, then just that knowledge is likely to affect the outcome of the trial. This phenomenon is very well-researched, a point that is made obvious by the fact that it would be much cheaper to test drugs in a more straightforward manner.

If the world of scientific research relies so heavily on a need to control the beliefs of the people in its studies, it's definitely a mistake for us to think that beliefs don't affect us as individuals. If you don't believe you have the power to reach your goals, or if you expect to fail, then I encourage you to deal with this issue before you start the physical part of weight loss again. To simply jump into the next protocol without addressing this problem first is to say, "What I believe is irrelevant. I'll be fine if I just get to work."

I'm sorry, but you probably won't be fine. Beliefs matter.

Chapter Sixteen
What Are the Stakes?

IN THEIR BOOK *The Confidence Code*, authors Katty Kay and Claire Shipman describe perfectionism in women with some very compelling examples. It seems that women might be more prone to be perfectionist in nature than men. Kay and Shipman say:

> But, of all the warped things that women do to themselves to undermine their confidence, we found the pursuit of perfection to be the most crippling. If perfection is your standard, of course you will never be fully confident, because the bar is always impossibly high, and you will inevitably and routinely feel inadequate.

> Moreover, perfectionism keeps us from action. We don't answer questions until we are totally sure of the answer, we don't submit a report until we've line edited it ad nauseam, and we don't sign up for that triathlon unless we know we are faster and fitter than is required. We watch our male colleagues lean in, while we hold back until we believe we're perfectly ready and perfectly qualified.

Perfectionism is almost always a bad thing, although some might tout it as a beneficial trait in business. Competence and attention to detail are excellent traits to bring to most tasks, but perfectionism is usually just another form of self-abuse. It is absolutely possible to do a job well without taking every opportunity to second-guess yourself.

When I bring all this information back to the subject of fat loss, the one thing that always jumps out at me is that women seem to believe that the stakes are much higher than they really are. Improving health and fat loss are, in fact, long-term, very slow processes in which each little choice you make, each habit you instill in yourself, produces a tiny benefit right now or in the very near future. Those tiny benefits add up to an awesome life, not just smaller pants. When you truly understand this, and when you address the various beliefs that I hope I'm helping you to see in yourself, you win.

So common is perfectionism that I've discussed this subject with more women than I could ever count. So many have come to me with a mentality that says, "If I can't do this perfectly, I'm not doing it at all." If a woman is thinking this way, she'll punish herself for every "mistake" instead of stepping back and looking at the big picture where she could see and assess her general movement in the right direction. This is the person who often has a very strong "dieting" mentality and is driven to follow the "rules" of this new thing she's doing. If she makes a misstep, she has a hard time moving past it.

So I'll ask you what I would ask her: What's at stake? What is there to be a perfectionist about?

Okay, maybe it is a fact that you are a perfectionist. I would overstep my knowledge and skill set if I claimed that I could help you change that fact in all aspects of your life, but there's no need to bring your perfectionism to your fat-loss goals. If it never makes you happy when you apply it to the areas of your life where it almost makes sense, then it definitely has no place at all here.

Think about it. What happens if you "fail" at a diet? Even if you completely give up and don't learn anything from the experience, you're not going to get fired when you go back into work the next day. Nobody is going to take your kids away or burn your house down. All the people who love you will still love you. Any and all anxiety over perfectionism in weight loss lies exclusively in your own head.

I can see why a person might find it hard to couch a perfectionist nature when it comes to a big project in her job. There could be big consequences, like unemployment, if she blows it and huge benefits, like raises and promotions, if she nails it. I get it; there really is a lot at stake in some situations, and even though perfectionism does not produce a tangible advantage while it usually does produce more stress, at least it's *more* rational in those high-stakes situations. But the stakes are basically nonexistent when it comes to personal fat-loss goals.

Make a list of things that will happen to you if you "fail" at your next fat-loss attempt. Seriously, I'm asking you to write out a list of the consequences. You can even include all the things you think you're missing out on by not having the body of your dreams. Then take a long, hard look at that list. I'm positive you will see that every item on it lives in your head and nowhere else.

There might be two exceptions, but neither change my point. First, your primary goal might truly be about health and not aesthetics. If you are in poor health, then the stakes really are high, but if so, you've probably been bored while reading this book so far because a focus on health negates almost all the things we've been talking about. Furthermore, a focus on health, with the proper dietary and exercise advice, will almost always produce fast improvements in the way you feel, so it's not hard to stay the course. Pain and misery are great motivators.

Second, you might be in a situation in which the worst kind of extrinsic motivation has been handed to you when someone you love said, "I'm walking out of your life if you don't lose weight." This might seem like a very high-stakes situation in which you have an "I need to lose weight to save my relationship" problem. In truth, you have an "I need to love myself enough to not let jackasses into my life" problem. Both are high-stakes problems, though. They're just very different problems. It's not my intention to be cavalier with your major life decisions, but you aren't currently in a good spot.

If you're the kind of person who worries about getting everything just right, I urge you to spend some time thinking about how that affects your fat-loss goals. Think about how perfectionism has helped you in the past. Have you been more successful because of your all-or-nothing belief? Or has that belief only caused you more frustration? If I were to venture a guess, I would say that you've needlessly suffered at the hands of your own self-imposed ideals about how the process of losing your unwanted fat should unfold. I don't think perfectionism helps anywhere in life, but if you're going to do it, do it in things with higher stakes than this, because it really is negatively affecting your ability to follow through. Which brings me to my next extremely important point.

Chapter Seventeen
Stop Stopping

OVERWHELMINGLY, THE PATTERN that I see among the women I work with looks like this:

1. She starts making lifestyle changes in an attempt to lose weight.
2. After a short time, usually no more than a few weeks, a "mistake" is made. For example, she might eat some cake at a wedding or a few pieces of her kids' Halloween candy.
3. The aforementioned mistake somehow "ruins" her preceding hard work as well as her future decisions. In short, she stops everything she was doing to lose weight.
4. After the arbitrary time spent off the rails, she begins to feel bad about her choices. "Why did I ever quit?!"
5. She starts again, but without ever addressing the real problem at hand.

When I started this chapter with the word "overwhelmingly," I actually meant OVERWHELMINGLY. Nothing is more common in my world than this pattern. The reason that so many people get stuck in this loop is that—you guessed it—they harbor the wrong beliefs.

If you are truly trying to get healthy, your efforts should be focused on creating new habits. Habits require practice. You aren't practicing anything if you quit every time you stumble. In order to get good at something, you have to do it often. What if you were learning to play a new musical instrument and you quit practicing for weeks each time you hit a sour note?

The real problem here is once again about motivations. Remember, if you're extrinsically motivated, you'll see the day-to-day procedures of fat loss as a cross to bear. You won't love the process, but rather think of it as something that must be endured to get what you ultimately want: a smaller body that other people will approve of. As such, you will look at healthy meals and workouts as things that must be strung together in order to produce something that can be assessed on your bathroom scale. In other words, you'll think, "I blew it when I ate that candy, so what's the point of making a good choice now?"

In contrast, let me challenge you with an example of an intrinsic motivation. What if I told you that you could only take one shower in the next month? I very seriously doubt that you would say, "One shower? Well, then screw it! That's not enough to make a difference. It takes at least 20 showers to make a difference!"

On the contrary, that one shower would be the best shower of your life! You would look forward to it, enjoy every moment of it, and remember it fondly when it was over. Why? Because you take showers for you. After coming home from a camping trip and a week of no showers, you don't need a few weeks to get motivated to shower again. Sure, bathing has the added benefit of making you not offend the noses of the people around you, but that's not really why you do it. Being more attractive is just the icing on the cake, just like being more attractive is the icing on the cake when we get healthy.

Here's a thought. What if you made a poor decision in a moment of weakness and you simply got back on track with the very next decision instead of throwing the baby out with the bathwater and giving up? What would happen? No need to imagine it; I'll tell you what would happen. At the end of a month of putting mistakes behind you immediately, you would have an abundance of days in which you were practicing your new lifestyle. You would be better at trying to figure out what to eat when you go to a restaurant. You would be better at navigating those temptations to sit on the couch instead of going for a walk. You would be better at turning off the television and going to bed at a reasonable hour. And, most importantly, you would be better at understanding yourself and the kinds of things that derail you.

You do absolutely need to string together some time living in a healthy fashion in order for your body to adapt to a new way of life and produce the changes you seek, but what good are you doing yourself if you can't even get to that point of consistency because you're too busy quitting with every mistake?

What I'm about to propose might sound crazy, but it's so important. If you're tempted by something, cupcakes for example, and your weight loss attempts come to a screeching halt every time you eat one, then focusing on avoiding cupcakes is actually the wrong tack. It makes much more sense to focus on your behavior *after* you eat a cupcake than it does to try to never eat another cupcake. Yes, you will need to avoid cupcakes to be successful. No, I am absolutely not giving you license to eat cupcakes with abandon. To return to our music example, you need to try to do everything in your power to avoid hitting sour notes, but you also need to continue to practice after it happens. Quitting solves nothing, unless your real goal was to feel bad about yourself.

Enough of the extrinsic motivations that never get you all the way to the finish line. Enough of the challenge diets that tell you you're a failure if you didn't make it 30 days without making a mistake, even though you were totally unprepared because you had no time to practice. A bad decision is a one-off event. It exists in isolation. Eating off plan at lunch has no more effect on dinner than Tuesday's shower has on Wednesday's. Just analyze your deviation, looking for ways to learn from it, and then keep moving.

Chapter Eighteen
There's No Such Thing as Monday

WHAT IS OUR fascination with Mondays? Look back over your whole life and I bet you can't find a single example of a goal you started on a Friday at 4 p.m. It's like an unwritten law that all diets and exercise plans must start on Monday morning. I take issue with this concept.

When we think about the actions involved with following a new plan, there is nothing inherently wrong with waiting until Monday to get started, but as is almost always the case, we overlook the psychological and behavioral impact of this common trend. As I've been demonstrating on these pages, psychology and behavior are the judge and jury overseeing the case of your fat-loss success or failure.

If you will, picture yourself on a Sunday afternoon in your local grocery store, where you happen to run into your good friend, Sally. She looks more vibrant and healthy than last time you saw her, so you ask her what she's been doing. She tells you she's been working with me (shameless self-promotion) and recommends that you read my work. You do the necessary reading over the next three days, finishing before bed on Wednesday. As you crawl in bed, you think, "That sounds like it might be what I've been looking for. I know I've said that before, but Sally looks great. I'll give it a go on Monday."

Sound familiar? Sure it does. We've all done it. But what happens between Wednesday night and Monday morning? Anticipation and maybe even anxiety that help to build your decision into something much bigger than it really is. You will remember from the last chapter that there's nothing of import at stake here. You could easily go back to the grocery store on Thursday, buy anything you need for the dietary changes and literally start as soon as you get home from the store. Instead, you spend a few days thinking about what you're going to have to do, getting your game face on, preparing to really give it your all this time, and imagining what you're going to look like in your amazing new body. You might even do some swimsuit shopping in your mind, or dig through your closet to find those old pants you've wanted to get back into.

If you're smelling what I'm stepping in, you can see that you're artificially raising the stakes of something that you could just start and do without all the emotion. Lifestyle change is a long, drawn-out process that must happen below your radar at times (more on this in the next chapter) and rote procedure needs to take the place of emotional impulse.

You may cry, "But what if I make a mistake?" So what? Learn as you go and don't repeat mistakes. If you nail it the first time around, our boys won't be magically coming home from war with you as their hero. If you choose a food that doesn't fit your plan, California won't fall into the ocean.

Forward motion is all that's required of you, and this is the other problem with waiting until Monday. If you allow yourself to be an "I'll start Monday" person, then you will probably also be a person who thinks that some arbitrary amount of time is ruined by your mistakes. For example, if you make a poor food choice at lunch, you become more likely to eat junk food at dinner because "today is already ruined." If you happen to make this poor choice on a Friday, you might even extend the correction out to your beloved

Monday morning, undoing who knows how much hard work over the weekend.

A much more effective approach will be to turn all of this "Monday" stuff into "right now" stuff. Through this perspective shift, you should find it a little easier to reduce the perceived magnitude of your goals and the things you're doing to reach them. All the ruminating and dwelling on the process and expected outcome is only serving to build things up into something they are not. Give yourself the chance to enjoy the process by remembering that you will always have all the control.

Screw Monday. Now is perfect.

Chapter Nineteen
"This Is So Exciting!"

NOTHING ABOUT THE pursuit of health and fat loss should ever be viewed as a temporary fix, so it's essential that you're focused on the long haul from the very beginning. This is much easier said than done, but it can save you a lot of frustration.

When someone first finds me, usually through a referral from a friend or family member, she is driven by excitement. She has seen results in others, and she jumps in with both feet. Before long, she starts seeing some results of her own. She joins our Facebook community and finds a new "us," she begins using our lingo and shorthand, and she enjoys a new group of friends to relate to and lean on for support. She might even buy our swag so she can proudly proclaim her dedication with a logo on a T-shirt.

Overall, lifestyle change often starts in much the same way as new hobbies do. There's so much fun in the newness of it all! There are new things to learn, new people to meet, and lots of new things to do. But lifestyles are not hobbies. Lifestyles require *being*, while hobbies require only *doing*.

I always feel like a party pooper when I ask newcomers, "What will you do when the excitement wears off?" When finding new recipes to fit your new way of eating loses its pizazz, will you keep eating that way? When you've had all the conversations you can possibly have about all the various subjects around your new lifestyle, will you stay the course? When most of your new friends have quit and fallen by the wayside, will you trudge on?

Here's one of the most important concepts I can ever ask you to get your head around: You need to be able to eat right and exercise properly in the same way that you take a shower and brush your teeth. You probably get excited about taking a shower only on those rare occasions when you're extra dirty or freezing cold, but you still bathe on all the other days, too. No excitement required. Why? Because the alternative is not an option. You brush your teeth each day because not brushing your teeth is unthinkable. You probably take a shower and brush your teeth at approximately the same time most days as well, because your grooming habits are just that: habits. They're part of who you are, not just something you're trying out for a while.

If I can't convince you to get to a place in your mind where the way you eat, move, sleep, and manage your stress is just part of who you are, then those things are activities for you and you're probably just passing through. Think about how many things in your life you've started and stopped. Most of us can make a fairly substantial list. We've tried lots of pastimes, hobbies, games, and sports. We check out different genres of books, different academic interests, and even different careers. And we quit most of these things when they become tedious or boring.

Why should fat-loss goals be any different? They're easy when they're fun and new, but then what? You have to be able to carry on when excitement is not there to fuel you anymore. In fact, most of your healthy lifestyle choices need to eventually happen under the radar of your conscious decisions. "I will exercise today because today is a workout day for me" is something that should be said with the same easy conviction as, "I will take a shower because it's morning." No extra thought or internal negotiations required.

Please note that I'm not suggesting that you "go hard or go home" or some other silly notion about not quitting when everyone else is weak and pathetic. That works in the beginning, but it's still driven by excitement. At some point you need to find yourself in a place where no emotion of any kind, either positive or negative, is involved in the way you live in your body. That's where the magic happens. If you think about it, you're living that way now. You aren't emotional about your current lifestyle, but it isn't producing health. To get healthy forever, you will eventually have to live a healthier lifestyle with the same lack of emotion.

I don't eat healthy foods with a specific outcome in mind anymore. I don't think, "I'm eating this dinner of steak and broccoli because I expect something to happen." I just eat it, and after hundreds and then thousands of meals, things have happened. Are those things exciting? Sure, I suppose they are when I really think about them, but the excitement is not the fuel that makes me live this way.

People who need excitement to continue with their fat-loss goals are people who jump ship a lot. They've done lots of different plans and followed lots of different gurus, all because diet and exercise are things that need to be engaging for them. Contrast that to being a human in nature, where acquiring food and moving were necessities. Getting up and going out into the world to find something to eat was a requirement, not a hobby.

The action step here is to know what you're after from the start. In the beginning, enjoy the excitement and use it to get through the early days when you need to learn a lot, but always keep in mind that it *will* be temporary. Since temporary results are not what you're shooting for, you should actively be trying to find the shortest path from *new and exciting* to *normal and habitual*. It's great to immerse yourself in something new. It's great to make new friends and feel like you're part of something bigger than you. It's great to hungrily devour all the new information you can get your hands on regarding your new lifestyle. But it's not great to be left standing there with that blasé feeling and no habits to fall back on when the excitement that got you this far has fizzled out.

Chapter Twenty
Your History Matters

AS WE'LL EXPLORE in more detail later, weight gain and loss are all about adaptation. Your body is an adaptation pro. This is fantastic for your survival, but not so great if you've spent years trying to lose weight through less-than-healthy means, especially starvation diets and excessive amounts of exercise designed to "burn" calories.

When driving down the number on your scale takes precedence over improving health, then metabolisms usually take a beating. Evidence of this can be seen in the fact that successive attempts at those kinds of fat-loss plans return worse and worse results. You starve yourself once and lose a bunch of weight, gain it right back, starve yourself again and lose less weight, gain it back (and usually more), starve yourself again and lose even less weight, and gain even more back. It's a vicious cycle that should have never made any sense to anyone, but alas, this is the most commonly prescribed advice in the world.

It is not my intent for this book to give you a lot of physical fat-loss advice, so why am I bringing this up here? Because your beliefs need to be adjusted if you have a long history of war with your body. Most people carry around at least a loose notion of what weight-loss diets and exercise should look like and what they should produce.

Right now, in your local bookstore, there are books with titles like *The Pound-a-Week Diet* (I think I made this one up, but I may be wrong). Most weight loss coaching companies, the kind in which you check in with a coach of some kind each week, have consistent weekly or monthly goals that you're supposed to hit if you want to call yourself successful on their plan.

All these things serve to instill in you the idea that fat loss should happen at a certain linear rate, and that such a rate can be compared with the rate that fat loss happens in others. When you believe this nonsense, you will use it to gauge your progress and the effectiveness of your efforts, and you will do so irrespective of what your body has already been through and the adaptations it was forced to make along the way. This mistaken assumption will almost ensure your long-term failure to reach your goals.

It probably makes intuitive sense that all bodies are different. That's one of those things that just sounds right, but it is also easily ignored. Even taking this into account, though, is not enough to fully understand the unpredictable path your body will take from here to peak health. The only part of that journey that you really have control over is the ability to give your body what it needs to be healthy.

If you've been treating your body like it's your enemy, it's definitely going to need some time to heal, but you don't get to decide which problems it fixes first. To your body, extra body fat is just one item on a list of repairs that need to be made. In fact, extra body fat is actually more of an indication of other problems than it is a problem in and of itself. There are lots of issues regarding thyroids, insulin sensitivity, and metabolic flexibility (to name a few) that must be addressed, and all of these things are almost always made worse by more years spent in traditional weight-loss pursuits.

I'm not telling you any of this to break your heart. What's done is done and you shouldn't dwell on it, but you *do* need to adjust your thinking accordingly. Our underlying theme of loving yourself enough to change for the right reasons is very appropriate here. Your body wants to be healthy, but you have to give it what it needs, every day, and then let it do its thing. Sometimes your short-term expectations will need to be quelled in favor of allowing your body to heal however it needs to.

Chapter Twenty-One
You Are Not the Exception

WHILE IT IS certainly true that every woman has her own body and her own history, and every body will respond a bit differently to a plan designed to improve health, there is no reason to convince yourself that you are the one person for whom nothing will ever work. The small details of progress come in various forms, but the big ones are rarely surprising to those of us with plenty of experience coaching fat loss.

The belief that your obstacles are unique to you is one that can take the wind out of your sails. Fortunately, it is a belief usually based on false premises. When you've done a lot of things that ended in something that felt like failure to you, and when you've seen examples of success in other people doing those same things, you might start feeling like you aren't normal. You might think, "I'm not like those people. Something is wrong with me that excludes me from the winner's club." In reality, there's nothing wrong with you at all. "Normal" doesn't really exist when it comes to fat-loss timelines. As such, all fat loss happens at a "normal" pace.

As the creator of a fat-loss diet, I've seen amazing testimonials produced in just a few weeks. I've seen my protocol produce shocking results in which some people seem to get whole new bodies in just a couple of months. Is this normal? Hell, no! I do my best to be the voice of reason when someone posts results like this on social media. I'll often say something like, "Congratulations on your awesome success. To everyone else reading this, these are not results that everyone can expect." Sadly, not every diet creator will lay down such a disclaimer, because those fast results sell lots of books. Even more sadly, many people will choose to ignore disclaimers, which is why extreme testimonials are so effective. When we see amazing results, we can so easily tune out the "results not typical" warning in the (subconscious) hope that we will be "not typical," too.

My point is that we see the fast and amazing results *because* they're fast and amazing, not because they're normal. When someone gets results like that, of course they want to share them with everyone. There's no harm in being excited about what really amounts to equal parts hard work and good fortune. The harm is in the rest of us believing that those stories are the results that everyone should expect.

It's important to understand that the very second you believe yourself to be an exception, you give away control. When you say, "Fat loss is harder for me than it is for other people," you've given yourself an excuse to fail. You've basically said, "When I fail, it will be because I am cursed with this inability to succeed."

I can absolutely assure you that there's nothing wrong with you that I haven't seen before, and I have seen every different kind of person succeed. Women with decades of unhealthy dieting in their past, women with eating disorders, women with thyroid issues or no thyroid at all, women in or after menopause, women with over 100 pounds to lose, women who didn't begin to pursue health until well after the age of 60, women with severe digestive issues, women with fibromyalgia, and even women with major diseases like multiple sclerosis, heart disease, and type 2 diabetes—I've seen them all get healthy, fit, and happy. While it is true that some of these things necessitate more diligence and patience, none of them makes success impossible, and none of them places you on an island all by yourself.

Unfortunately, I've seen many more people settle into these obstacles, making them part of their identity and annihilating any hope of ever reaching their goals. In truth, most will never get too far beyond the starting line. This is a victim mentality, and once it takes root, it almost always wins the day. Whatever cards you have been dealt, they're playable. Pull up a chair and get back in the game.

Chapter Twenty-Two
"But You Have to Be Happy!"

A COMMON COMPLAINT: "I understand trying to make healthier food choices, but you can't be suggesting that I give up _____ (usually sugar or some other form of junk food) forever, because that would just be ridiculous. You have to be happy!" I've got nothing but tough love for this one.

What the hell does ice cream have to do with happiness? Any emotional eater can tell you that eating to find happiness has *never* worked. Not even once. You don't come home from a bad day at work, eat a chocolate bar, and suddenly your boss wasn't an ass all day. In fact, not one of your worries or stresses was ever alleviated by eating any kind of food in one meal, unless hunger was your biggest problem at the time. Eating junk food has even less to offer because it doesn't even leave you feeling better physically.

I once polled my clients and online followers about emotional eating, asking them how long the elation lasts when they eat junk food after a bad day. The average answer was 30 seconds. Some said they already felt guilty as they were taking the first bite, which negated any positive effect they were hoping for.

We talked about this earlier, but it's important to remember that when you eat highly palatable foods in the hope that they will make you happy, you're chasing a dopamine hit. Since dopamine is a *wanting* hormone, not a *liking* hormone, it's designed to make you repeat things that are supposed to be good for you, not make you enjoy those things when you're doing them and then leave you feeling happy afterward. In other words, the effects are very short-lived by evolutionary design, and happiness is not involved in the equation.

You're not supposed to stay happy after a dopamine response; you're supposed to repeat whatever gave it to you. In nature, food that tasted good was good for you, but we have very effectively broken that rule in our modern world with foods like cheesecake that have very little nutritional value and that nobody eats when she's actually hungry.

This obstacle is an emotional objection that's not based on any-thing rational. Since junk food has never really made anyone happy, and since it's especially unlikely to make you happy if eating it means betraying your fat-loss goal, then there is nothing substantial behind the belief that eliminating junk food will also eliminate a source of happiness. We can take this a step further and say that eliminating junk food will also not negatively affect existing happi-ness by making you more unhappy. I have searched the world over for a counterpoint to this argument, and I can't find one.

Emotional eating is real, and it's not my intention to belittle emo-tional eaters, but it does not work to improve happiness. If you currently hold the belief that sugar, for example, is affecting your happiness in any way, then I implore you to give that belief some close inspection. I think you'll find that it falls short of logical. Sim-ply changing this belief will probably not change your desire for sugar—there's more to it than that—but it will arm you with a ra-tional line of thinking that you can use to mindfully change course when you're tempted. "Why am I about to do something that has literally never worked for me?"

Chapter Twenty-Three
The "What Can I Get Away With" Mentality

THERE'S A COMMON theme that runs deep among those who are extrinsically motivated. When you believe that the world wants you to lose weight, and when you feel like something grandiose will happen to you when you do, you're not driven by anything inside you, but rather by what you believe you'll receive from others. Understandably, you'll look for the path of least resistance in your lifestyle changes.

Certain questions are huge red flags for me when I begin working with someone new. Many people ask, "Okay, but how often can I have pizza and still lose weight? Once a week?" Or, "How many glasses of wine can I have each week? I have to be able to unwind after work, so just tell me how much wine is allowed on this plan."

When I hear questions like this, I always respond by saying, "I don't think you're ready for this right now." This never goes over well, but I don't have another worthwhile answer. This is a person who is not at all focused on what she's going to gain, and that tells me that she probably doesn't really believe she can be successful. I'm inclined to think that anyone who believes beyond the shadow of a doubt that she *will* succeed would gladly trade a weekly pizza for those results, especially if she's intrinsically motivated to get healthy and fit for herself because she knows she deserves it.

The "What can I get away with?" mentality screams, "My comfort zones are more important to me than my goals!" I am by no means saying that occasionally eating pizza or drinking wine will derail everyone, but I am saying that the belief that these things are important and should be guarded and cherished is not one that's conducive to successful fat loss.

A better perspective is one that focuses on what will be gained. "Sure, I'm giving up a glass of wine each evening, but I look forward to feeling so much better as I get healthier and more physically capable."

This is not just an issue of semantics. If you think in terms of what you're giving up to get healthy and do everything in your power to not give up an ounce more than necessary, then you are absolutely not properly motivated. You don't need another failure to hold against yourself later, so why start something that you're destined to quit? To say, "I like my life exactly the way it is," is also to say, "I don't like what I'm going to have to do to reach my goals." This needs fixing. When it comes to sustainable fat loss, half-assed efforts don't produce half-assed results, they produce temporary, short-term results or no results at all.

It's okay to walk away, fix your perspective, and come back when you can win. That's one of the central themes of this whole book!

Chapter Twenty-Four
"Just Tell Me What to Do and I'll Do It"

ANOTHER PERSPECTIVE THAT usually causes prob-
lems if it isn't adjusted along the way comes from people who want
a list of rules to follow, kind of like a fat-loss itinerary. The belief
here goes back to the idea that fat loss happens when we simply do
certain things without changing who we are. To impress this upon
you for not the last time, that is a bad assumption. Major lifestyle
changes always run deeper than just a set of action steps.

These folks are usually in a better place than those who are looking
for what they can get away with or those who think they need
flavor to be happy, but this is still a genuine obstacle because this
"Just tell me what to do and I'll do it" mentality demonstrates a
lack of ownership of the process. It basically says, "I don't want to
think about any of this stuff; I just want to change my body."
Unfortunately, ownership is almost always required for long-term
success.

Very few people will be able to follow a to-do list and get all the
way to the finish line. One reason for this is that a list won't
prepare you for those inevitable times when you have to make
tough choices. For example, if you are at a party where there is only
one option that is on your list of acceptable foods, do you pig out
on that one dish to the detriment of the other guests? Do you eat a

small amount and potentially not meet some other guidelines of your protocol, like total daily calories? Do you fast for the evening?

If you need to think on the fly once in a while, which you certainly will, you'll be much better equipped to do so if you harbor the belief that every day and every situation is another opportunity to learn and refine your healthy new lifestyle. In this situation, a belief that planning your journey to health is someone else's problem will put you at an immediate deficit.

There's one place where this mentality is generally not a problem. When it comes to exercising with a personal trainer, you can rely on your trainer to tell you what to do and when to do it because you aren't ever exercising on your own, or at least not without your trainer prescribing your workouts. This situation is different because you aren't likely to be at a social event where everyone breaks into a new kind of squat you've never seen before, placing you at risk of injury for your lack of knowledge.

Take ownership of your goals and the methods you're using to achieve them. Learn as much as you can and assess your own attitudes, behaviors, and beliefs along the way. It is a mistake to assume that lifestyle change happens by stepping where someone tells you to step without any other considerations. New habits must be created, ideals and preferences must change, and you will need to turn new choices into a new you.

Chapter Twenty-Five
Rewards

AFTER MAKING GOOD choices for a solid week or three, you will be proud of your resolve, and rightfully so. Changing habits is hard! It takes real dedication to make the kind of changes you're making. Maybe you *deserve* a piece of cake at that office birthday party!

Hold on there! What you're doing is something the psychologists call *moral licensing*, and it's another nasty little pitfall.

Moral licensing, in this case, is when you tell yourself that you've been doing so well with your dietary changes that you deserve to deviate off plan. In other words, you justify doing something in direct opposition to your goals by telling yourself that you're doing so well with your goals. It sounds silly when I word it like that, right?

Moral licensing usually comes with a side of "Besides, a little won't hurt anyway." This statement is correct only if you frame it just right. While it is true that one piece of birthday cake never made anyone fat, one badly timed piece of birthday cake has derailed more fat-loss attempts than we could ever tally. This is an important concept, and we will dig into the heart of it later, but for now, let's think about what you "deserve" when you've been "good."

Personally, when I feel like I'm kicking ass at life, I deserve better than flavor. When I'm being a good fat-loss coach, business owner, husband, dad, or health enthusiast, I deserve more of the things that truly contribute to my happiness, like time with my kids or a date with my wife. Maybe I've been working hard and I deserve some time in my favorite chair with a good movie. Whatever I choose, it's always better than junk food. I can't imagine what task I would have to accomplish that would be so pathetically small that the reward would be a piece of cake. Everything I do that makes me feel good about myself is worth more to me than that.

Don't you feel the same? If someone said, "Great job, here's a cookie," wouldn't you think, "Thanks, but I'm not four years old"?

This seems even sillier to me when I think about working really hard at something and then rewarding myself by doing the opposite of what I have been working so hard at. I couldn't imagine raking all the leaves in my yard and then rewarding myself by spreading some leaves back over a small patch. I wouldn't hit myself in the thumb with a hammer because I had been doing so well at not hitting my thumb with my hammer. I wouldn't say, "Wow, I have really done a great job cleaning this house! I'm going to go get a handful of dirt and spread it around the living room, because I deserve it!"

Okay, I know, I'm being facetious. But these examples are off-base only if you believe that eating junk food will provide some sort of benefit to your life. Since you know in your heart that it won't, why deliberately turn and move in the opposite direction of all your hard work and then try to call it a reward?

Have you ever said, "I worked my butt off for an extended period of time, and I am so proud of my progress, but I made the best decision I've made in a long time when I decided to undo some of that hard work and return to the behavior that used to make me miserable"? Of course not!

When we examine moral licensing in this light, it's pretty clear that it starts with a false belief and ends with a quick emotional decision. If we know what it is and we recognize it when it shows itself, moral licensing is more easily defeated. I'm not suggesting that you'll never be tempted to derail yourself ever again just because I've explained a new psychology term to you, but you should find it much harder to rationalize a poor choice by telling yourself that you deserve a treat. There are much better rewards than guilt and rot gut. Go do something that won't leave you feeling bad in the end. That's what you deserve.

Chapter Twenty-Six
Change Is Hard, but Not as Hard as Not Changing

THE BELIEF THAT change is hard is absolutely accurate. We are creatures of habit. Our brains do whatever they can to relegate as much of our lives as possible to habit so that we don't have to be actively using brain power all day long for every little thing we do.

When you were first learning how to drive, for example, you had to think about every action—how hard to press the pedals, how far the steering wheel needed to turn if you wanted to make a corner, when to turn on your turn signal when changing lanes—but now you can drive home from work while your mind wanders the whole way. We don't tend to keep track of such things, but it was probably only after a month or two of regular driving that you had formed habits solid enough to allow you to daydream your way through a trip.

Fortunately, driving isn't something that we learn while fending off massive temptations to not drive. Getting healthy has many more potential obstacles, yet it still requires us to form habits if we hope to be successful. That means holding a new pattern for what could seem like an eternity if you're struggling.

Yes, change is very hard, and healthy lifestyle change might be among the hardest changes a person can make. I won't try to tell you how easy it will be for you while I wave my pom-poms and jump into the splits (sorry about that visual). If you're overweight and in less-than-stellar health, the road from there to a fabulous body that will last you a lifetime is uphill, slippery, and filled with ruts.

However, I'd like to propose a counterpoint. As hard as it might be to change your lifestyle and get the body you want, isn't it much harder to not change?

If you do choose to dig in and do what you need to do, you'll have to change the way you eat. That will require overcoming temptations every day, developing new tastes, and learning how to prepare new foods. You'll have to make time to move your body each day and then do it even when it's hard. You'll have to prioritize sleep and manage your stress, despite the fact that those things will take even more of your valuable time and force you to give up even more of the things you find so comfortable and enjoyable right now. You'll have to stay consistent with all of this even though the results are guaranteed to come slowly and in small doses. And you'll almost assuredly have to work as hard to change your head as you do to make all those other changes combined.

It might sound much easier to not change, but is it? Is it easy to see your reflection and have it ruin your day? Is it easy to say things to yourself that you would never have the guts to say to someone you don't like, let alone a friend? Is it easy to go clothes shopping and leave frustrated? Is it easy to suffer from anxiety about an upcoming tropical vacation rather than just being excited? Is it easy to worry that you might be teaching your daughter to be like you? Is it easy to go to such lengths to make sure that the person who loves you never sees you naked under good lighting? Is it easy to spend so much of your life worrying about how you look and what other people think about you?

If none of these things is an issue for you, then you either are
intrinsically motivated to change for all the right reasons, or you
legitimately have valid reasons for not changing. Either way, these
are worthwhile questions.

I have worked with many women who, when we get past the face
that they show the world, are truly suffering inside based on what
they believe they are. Yet, when we start talking about the things
that will fix their misery, they understandably begin to feel overwhelmed by the enormity of it all. In my experience, perspective is
the best way around this obstacle. Yes, the job is a big one, but it
pales in comparison to living with such angst, frustration, and
sadness.

When you're feeling overwhelmed, never forget those things that
you suffer through each day. Even if almost all of them are self-
imposed, the pain is real. You don't have to hurt.

Chapter Twenty-Seven
Fat as an Identity

I AM A fat-loss coach. I am also 6 feet tall. One of those things is totally within my power to change, and the other is not. If I chose to, I could throw in the towel on this career tomorrow. I could shut off my website, YouTube channel, and social media pages, quit recording podcasts, and just sleep in every day. And I would stay 6 feet tall the whole time.

My height is part of who I am. My job is part of who I am right now.

When you say, "I'm fat," what do you *really* mean? If you've spent a large portion of your life trying to lose weight, then you may believe that your weight is an immutable part of who you are. You may have absorbed your body fat into your identity. If so, this is a problem that should be addressed if you ever hope to change forever.

Take a look around your life. People who believe themselves to be losers almost always eventually fail, even after so much success. People who believe themselves to be winners always seem to find a way, even when they appear to fail over and over again. Once again, it's easy to find evidence that what we believe becomes substantive over time.

If you truly believe that you're a fat person, rather than someone who's fat right now, you are likely to return to this condition regardless of what you ever try to do to change. It's as if your fatness is your home base of operations. You can occasionally leave, but you'll be back soon.

In your subconscious mind, you probably have some kind of loose template of the behaviors that make up a fat person—a script, if you will. A fat person is always talking about her weight with the people close to her. She's always insecure about her appearance. She's always dieting. She hates clothes shopping. She avoids her reflection. She hates having her picture taken. She blows off compliments. She seeks approval. There might be many more behaviors on your list, but you get the idea.

If you believe you're a fat person, you will use yourself and all the other fat people you've ever met to form an identity type. You'll see a common thread between you and the other people who seem to be like you. This all makes perfect sense. It only becomes problematic when you apply permanence.

Here's another example: If you went to college, you might have struggled with a hard class load while looking around at other students like you, all of you going through the same rigors, and thought, "It is really tough to be a college student." However, you powered through, busting your butt and passing your classes because "college student" was something you were going through, not something you believed you would be forever. If you held no hope of escaping that title, you would not have tried very hard to graduate. When you didn't do well on an exam, you would not think, "Okay, I clearly need to buckle down and learn as much as I can so I don't fail this class." On the contrary, you would think, "This poor grade makes perfect sense because, woe is me, I am a college student and will be doing this forever. Passing is not an option for me like it is for other people."

When I work with someone who truly believes she is a fat person and not just a person who's fat right now, we slam into that obstacle over and over again. So many of the things we've already talked about—self-sabotage, moral licensing, low confidence and self-worth, lack of an internal locus of control—will perpetually rear their ugly heads each time we make some progress, because changing an identity is much harder than changing the current condition of a body. It's frustrating for both of us—for her because she can't win and for me because I can see how she easily could win if she would just get out of her own way. The only way to win is to change her belief.

Unfortunately, this is one of those concepts that's easy to acknowledge but hard to own. A lifetime of belief won't go away because you understand it now. You'll have to work hard to change it, and we'll get to that, but you need to take some time to think about your own thought processes.

You might be tempted to say, "Well, I keep trying to lose weight, so I clearly think I can change. I obviously don't believe that 'fat person' is my identity, or I wouldn't keep doing new diets." Okay, but what does your inner voice say when you fail? When a diet doesn't work for you like it did for the people in the testimonials, or when you get some results and then gain all the weight back, what happens in your head? Do you buckle down and learn everything you can, putting yourself back on the path to success like you did in college? Or do you feel hurt and broken for a long while, listening to your inner voice telling you that this is where you belong? You might say things like, "These are the cards I've been dealt. I just have a slow metabolism."

I've seen every kind of body change forever when the head driving it takes the right kind of ownership and abandons the wrong kind. You should absolutely own responsibility for your current condition *and* your control over it, but you should not own your fat as an identity.

Chapter Twenty-Eight
The Fat Loss Stages of Change

PSYCHOLOGY PROFESSOR JAMES Prochaska developed the "transtheoretical model" of behavior change and wrote about it for the general public in his book *Changing for Good* (co-authored by John Norcross and Carlo DiClemente). The model describes six stages that we pass through, and sometimes return to, as we change a behavior. The stages are as follows:

- **Precontemplation:** A person in this stage is not even thinking about changing yet.
- **Contemplation:** A person in this stage is beginning to recognize something she wants to change and weighing the cost of following through.
- **Preparation:** A person in this stage is getting ready to begin the process of changing.
- **Action:** A person in this stage is doing the work of changing.
- **Maintenance:** A person in this stage has been maintaining the action stage for at least six months without backsliding.
- **Termination:** A person in this stage has changed. Temptation to return to old habits is gone.

When we apply this widely accepted model to fat loss, it becomes clear that we so often misunderstand how change happens, and we expect to be able to break the rules. I firmly believe that emotion and desperation are the cause of our blindness. Let's walk through the stages as they might unfold for a woman with a fat-loss goal.

<u>Precontemplation:</u> *"Fat loss? No, I'm fine."*

This woman doesn't have a fat-loss goal. We don't need to linger here, because I doubt that anyone reading this book will be in this stage.

<u>Contemplation:</u> *"I'm not happy with my body. Maybe I should try to lose some weight."*

Tens of millions of people are in this group right now. These are the frustrated folks who either haven't tried changing yet or are convinced that they never could. I don't encounter a lot of these people in my career because they don't seek me out, but they exist in huge numbers in every community in the Western world. Sadly, I believe the majority are in the hopeless camp.

Without a desire to start trying to change or the belief that you have a choice, obviously nothing will happen. This stage is not one I can help with. Not once have I ever given anyone a reason to get healthy and lean. The reasons that lead to success always come from within you.

<u>Preparation:</u> *"I'm going to try to lose weight. I just need to get my ducks in a row first."*

Preparing to begin a fat-loss plan, in my opinion, should be a very short stage, but we've already discussed a few reasons why it is often a long, drawn-out process. Many people spend way too much time here, either without moving past this stage or by continuously returning to it after brief periods of action.

When someone has a solid plan that could actually work to produce sustainable fat loss, one common reason she might get stuck in the Preparation stage is perfectionism. Many women will tell themselves that if they can't overhaul their lifestyle completely, perfectly applying every little piece of advice from someone like me with the flip of a switch, then they will have failed.

Since lifestyle change is hard and requires lots of small steps that add up to really big ones, perfectionists can get stuck at the starting line. When they do begin the work of changing, they simply expect too much of themselves. The realization that they have bitten off more than they can chew makes them feel weak or incapable, and they jump back into Preparation as quickly as they can before their inner voice beats them senseless. Nobody wants to feel like a failure, but the perfectionist's definition of "pass/fail" in this instance is the real problem. Trying to convince a perfectionist to try baby steps is like pulling teeth, but nothing is more effective for them.

While perfectionism is certainly anything but rare, it's not the most common problem that I see keeping people in the Preparation stage. By far, the biggest things knocking people back out of the Action stage are bad information and a lack of understanding of what fat loss truly is.

Tricks and gimmicks are everywhere, and very few people seem to inherently understand that sustainable fat loss will always be about improving health. As such, nearly everyone buys into ridiculous and oversimplified ideas when they try to lose weight. For example, the idea that food goes into a body and is either "burned" or stored as fat causes people to vilify food in general. Starvation diets ensue, but they are never sustainable, so everyone is constantly starting over. After enough attempts at starvation, a person might try attacking the perceived problem from the other side with copious amounts of exercise, but the results will be the same.

These two methods—cutting calories or doing lots of cardio—comprise the entire fat loss knowledge base of most of the world.

And, each time they fail, the people using them are thrust back into the Preparation stage.

However, even with a good plan, very few can keep themselves in the Action stage for long because of so many of the things we've been talking about in this book. Desperation, emotional attachment to the outcome, and the wrong motivations are compounded by self-loathing and low confidence, among other things, to create insurmountable obstacles. If your head is constantly tripping you up, you can probably look back over what you would describe as "a life of dieting" and see that you spent just as much time in the Preparation stage as you did actually doing the various plans you passed through. In fact, if you're average in that regard, you probably spent even more time in Preparation, because most people won't diligently stick with a plan for more than three weeks without falling off the wagon and starting again.

Although fewer in number, there are also those people who will get stuck in analysis paralysis. If you must know everything there is to know about fat loss before you begin, then you will never begin. I still learn every day. I have seen some extreme versions of this in which people literally become experts on the subject without changing themselves at all. If you look closely, it isn't hard to find dietitians with eating disorders and trainers with exercise addictions. I'm not talking about people who overcame a serious issue to become an expert with a wonderful testimonial; I'm saying there are plenty of professionals out there who have yet to change themselves.

My theory is that analysis feels like action to some people. They aren't actually applying their knowledge to themselves, but the process of learning more and more all the time is *almost* like traversing the path to their goals. If you convince yourself that reading three studies on mitochondrial function is the same as going for a walk and making healthier food choices, then you are probably going to be here for a while.

Action: *"No more messing around; it's time to do this!"*

The Action stage is where the work of losing weight happens, which means it is the hardest stage to stick to. All the temptations to quit happen here. To be clear (and redundant), nobody can be successful with a weight-loss plan that doesn't improve health, so most plans offer only a temporary stop in this stage before returning you to Preparation.

For the sake of argument, let's pretend you have an amazing plan already. Unfortunately, if amazing plans were all that were required for fat-loss success, I wouldn't have needed to write this book. Alas, successful Action stages happen almost exclusively through head changes—and preferably head changes that are made before the physical process of the amazing fat-loss plan ever begins.

According to the transtheoretical model, to call an Action stage successful, you have to remain there for six months. This is extra tricky with fat-loss goals, because you've been taught by a broken weight-loss industry that results should come quickly and should be linear in nature, producing consistent results from week to week and month to month. Since progress is actually unpredictable and unique to each person, you will get lots of false opportunities to label yourself a failure and quit. Add the slightest hint of desperation to the equation, and six months will feel like six decades.

In my experience, Prochaska is dead on with this milestone. Diligently sticking to a solid plan for six months almost always produces permanent change in some capacity. Even with not-so-great plans (as long as health isn't dramatically reduced), people tend to learn a lot about themselves and what they're capable of in six months. It becomes much easier to reduce desperation and focus on experimentation that eventually leads to success.

Maintenance: *"I got this."*

In the Maintenance stage, lifestyle changes have become habitual. Life might still require some occasional thought and planning, but the stress of the daily application is gone.

People in this stage are obviously fewer in number than in all the preceding stages, but they are not really rare. What does become rare about them is their narrative. These people are mostly done talking about what they're doing. Some stay active in social media groups that support others on the same plan, but they aren't spending a lot of time talking about their own experience anymore. They have a new lifestyle, and excitement isn't required for them to live it.

The things that take people out of the Maintenance stage and push them all the way back to Preparation are usually fairly substantial. Big life events that rob us of hope are still potential pitfalls at this stage. The death of a loved one, the end of a relationship, depression, and major financial stress are all capable of making anyone say, "Screw all this!" I understand completely. Sometimes life deals us cards that we just aren't strong enough to play in that moment. However, barring catastrophe, the Maintenance stage is a fine place to find yourself.

Termination: *"I remember a time when I struggled with my body."*

The Termination stage is the fat-loss Promised Land. All the *doing* is gone, replaced only with *being*. A person in this stage has become something new. The lifestyle she lives is so normal to her as to require no internal debate, and temptation is not an issue. For example, she might consider *when* she will exercise, but not *if*. She looks at pizza the way a nonsmoker looks at a pack of cigarettes. She recognizes all the amazing benefits that her lifestyle has delivered to her, not just her pants size, and she can't imagine jeopardizing those things for anything as trivial as flavor.

I won't say it isn't possible, but I have personally never seen anyone fall out of this stage. Even when the most horrible life events
happen, these people keep making healthy choices exactly the same
way that they continue to bathe and brush their teeth. You don't
think about the process of getting yourself ready to leave your
home in the morning, and these people don't think about the process of choosing healthy foods and getting to bed at a reasonable
hour.

Another thing I've seen in each person who reaches the
Termination stage is the awareness of her growth. She will always
tell me about the massive perspective shifts she has undergone to
get to where she is today. She started this journey trying to change
the way her body looks, but now all she talks about is the difference in her thinking. Even when she doesn't say the word "happy,"
it's writ large in her eyes.

It was when I finally realized what I was seeing in these women
that so many things started to click into place for me in my career.
This was the realization that made me say for the first time, "My
job isn't about bodies; it's about minds."

Chapter Twenty-Nine
The Definition of "Worked"

LET'S COMBINE TWO things that we've learned so far:

1. Sustainable fat loss happens only through improved health.
2. Change happens when the Action stage of the transtheoretical model of change is maintained for at least six months.

After considering these two facts, have you ever done a fat loss plan that worked? I'll assume that if you could answer *yes* to this question, you wouldn't be reading this book.

When I ask virtually anyone who has a history of yo-yo dieting to tell me about the various things she's done to lose weight, I almost always hear about one or two things that "worked" for her. She'll say something like, "I did Diet X for a couple of months and lost 20 pounds. I gained all the weight back when it got too hard, but it really worked for a while."

We need to redefine the word "worked" in this context. If you're overweight, then nothing in your past worked unless your *only* reason for quitting was based solely on your psychological state at the time. But don't be fooled: If the plan you were using was aimed at weight loss alone without very deliberately and obviously improving your overall health, then your wistful desire to return to those temporary results is a pipe dream. Plans like that do not "work."

Simply getting smaller for a while is not success. Successful fat loss is permanent.

If you can ever hope to steer clear of the shysters and scam artists who comprise the bulk of my industry, you must get your head around this concept. Temporary results are easy to create. If you do a crazy cleanse or starvation diet and get temporary results, only to regain all your lost weight and assume it's all your fault, you are exactly what the weight loss "experts" want you to be: someone who will gobble up their garbage and never place the blame on them.

There is no wiggle room with this belief. Fortunately, this is an easy one to change because you don't have to do anything other than know in your heart that real fat loss is permanent and will never happen through a trick or gimmick. You haven't overlooked anything, like a magical shake that "melts fat away" for just $500 a week. There isn't a class down at your local gym that, when attended six times a week, will make the Weight-Loss Fairy appear and grant all your wishes.

If you lose weight, you have to be able to keep it off with the same plan that took it off in the first place. At no point should that plan start to become deleterious to your health. If it does, then you were never doing anything sustainable in the first place. Failure was always imminent.

Believe it.

Chapter Thirty
The Maze

IF I'VE CONVINCED you that sustainable fat loss is about getting really healthy, and if getting really healthy requires diligence, consistency, and patience, then you should also be able to understand the importance of staying in the game without getting frustrated. One belief that stands in the way of consistency is that in which little obstacles are seen as impassable instead of opportunities to learn. Here again, it's an emotional attachment to the outcome that does the damage to your perspective.

When we make decisions rationally rather than emotionally, we can continue on our course indefinitely because we will stop labeling our decisions as right or wrong and start seeing the valuable information that they produce. Here's an analogy that illustrates my point:

You're standing at the entrance of a huge hedge maze. Immediately inside, you're faced with three possible paths. You choose to go right. Not so shockingly, your choice doesn't result in a straight shot to the exit, and after making a few twists and turns, you end up at a dead end. Since you fully expected to have to apply some brain power to make it through this thing, you simply return to the last intersection and make a different choice. Sitting down and crying at the dead end or leaving the maze entirely aren't options that you're willing to consider. You also inherently understand that you haven't done anything *wrong* unless you choose this same path again and expect it to lead to your goal.

Back at the intersection, you decide to take the left path this time. In doing so, you know that you're going to gain even more information, but you don't expect this path to lead straight to the exit, either. Yet, knowing that there will be more information and more decisions to make does not hinder your confidence that you'll find your way out eventually. Since you aren't passing any dead bodies along the way, you know that others have made it through this maze, and you will, too. You also know that nobody made it through by giving up.

You're capable of navigating a hedge maze because you can see it as a series of small problems that need to be solved, and you're acting rationally instead of emotionally. You might react very differently in a life-threatening situation, but traversing a hedge maze is usually not an emergency, and neither is fat loss.

If we pretend that the process of fat loss is like a maze, we can clearly see the mistakes we make. Maybe you've been down that same dead-end path numerous times instead of learning more about your body and moving on. Maybe you sat down and cried or exited the maze for months or years after finding only one dead end. Or two. Or three.

Some mazes have dozens of dead ends, but you would never see them as failures or mistakes. You just keep puzzling it out and looking for the exit that you absolutely know is there somewhere. Since you probably aren't too concerned about being judged for your ability to navigate a hedge maze, the whole process is just fun.

If you're like most people, you go through life not paying much attention to other people's bodies, but you tend to think that the whole world is acutely focused on yours. Fat loss becomes more

difficult when we, first, mistakenly believe that we're overly important and everyone is watching us and, second, when we become so
emotionally attached to the outcome of our endeavor that we do
silly things that we would never do if emotions weren't involved.
Emotions don't help with fat-loss goals, and they have to be force-
fully removed.

Without an inner voice to comment on every little step, fat loss is
just a learning process where patience and diligence prevail. How
do you combat your inner voice? We're almost there.

Chapter Thirty-One
What Are You Saying?

TIME FOR MORE questions. How do you talk to yourself? Do you think kind thoughts when you see yourself in a mirror?

Let's do a little experiment. The next time you see your closest girl-friend, I'd like you to talk to her *exactly* like you talk to yourself. It should probably play out something like this:

"Ugh, you look so fat today. That shirt is making it worse. Don't you have anything else to wear? Sheesh, you really need to get your butt in the gym. Your thighs are just gross!"

Then, when she sits across from you at lunch, avoid looking at her at all costs. In fact, maybe you could throw a towel over her like you might a free-standing mirror in your bedroom while you get dressed in the morning. If she does catch your eye for some reason, get right back to searching for more physical "flaws" that she might have, and be sure to tell her about everything you find.

This behavior breaks my heart. You would absolutely never treat another human being this way. Interestingly, *you* are the only person who would ever treat you this way. Whatever you believe everyone is thinking about you, whatever horrible judgments you *assume* they're making, *nobody* talks to you like you talk to you. Even if you have broken your life filter and let terrible people into your life who say terrible things to you, I guarantee that your inner voice is worse.

You might have a relatively healthy inner voice, but all of us sometimes take liberties with the respect that we show ourselves. Even those among us with the healthiest perspectives still occasionally judge ourselves more harshly than others ever would.

I understand the logic behind the advice to say five nice things to yourself in the mirror each morning, and maybe you should. But, if I'm being honest, I don't think you'll find a lot of lasting help there. My problem with that plan lies in the fact that it takes so many compliments to undo one insult. Take social media, for example. You post a photo of yourself and 50 people tell you that you look beautiful, but one person says you have bags under your eyes. That one negative comment instantly eradicates the 50 compliments. You won't think about all those sweet friends and their kind words all day. On the contrary, you'll probably head straight to a mirror to see if there's anything you can do to cover up those bags. And that one negative comment was probably worded in a way that doesn't even come close to the way we word these things when we are talking to ourselves.

Therefore, reciting, "I have nice hair. I like my smile. I have…" in a fashion that feels forced probably doesn't undo the damage of an inner voice that feels honest in that moment. You might be paying yourself compliments that you actually mean, but they lack the passion that you used to lash out at yourself only moments before. Again, I can't say that this exercise is completely useless, but I also don't believe that long-term change will happen there.

Journaling is another exercise that might have some small benefit for altering these horrendous thought patterns, but the results are probably similar to the self-complimenting thing. The problem with these kinds of exercises, in my opinion, is that they attempt to compete with the negative inner dialogue rather than change it.

Pushing back against your inner voice is fantastic, don't get me wrong, but the end result of your efforts should be to make it change its tone entirely. In my experience, creating a louder positive voice in your head, while certainly an improvement, is not as good as creating new thought patterns altogether.

If you have lived with brutal insults in your head for many years—and many women will say it's been a lifetime—you probably think I'm insane for suggesting that something so massive, so part of who you are, can be changed. But it can.

Chapter Thirty-Two
Rewiring

WE ARE WHAT we practice.

If you were to use an fMRI to examine the brain of cello virtuoso Yo-Yo Ma while he plays Bach, you would see very distinct pathways of electricity in his brain. If you then examined a beginner cellist playing the same piece, the difference in the activity of the two brains would be dramatic.

What we're talking about here is *myelination*. Myelin is the stuff your brain creates and uses like the plastic insulation around electrical wires. Since all thoughts are basically just electrical currents traveling between synapses, myelin helps keep those currents on track. As such, the actions or thought patterns that you practice the most, like Yo-Yo Ma playing the cello, are represented by highly myelinated pathways in your brain.

I repeat, we are what we practice. You probably aren't a world-class cellist, but you might happen to be someone who's spent many years practicing a thought pattern that says, "That person over there just looked at me, and now they clearly think I'm fat." If so, that process is now automatic. When you meet new people, making assumptions about what they think of your body comes as naturally to you as the feel of the bow in his hand does to Yo-Yo Ma. That pathway *will* be your knee-jerk response forever if you don't do something to change it.

The way that almost everyone will address this problem is to give substance to these negative thoughts. You don't really know what anyone else is thinking, but your own thoughts seem so real that the desperate pursuit of weight loss at all costs ensues as you try to change what you're guessing are the thoughts of other people. This is a fight that absolutely nobody can win without a head change, but very few will ever make anything more than a momentary, half-hearted effort to change their heads.

Well, I'm putting my foot down. Let me be perfectly clear:

You CANNOT succeed without changing your perspective.
It WILL be hard.
It WILL take months.
You MUST do it anyway.

Think of the countless hours, days, weeks, months, and years that you've already spent doing various things to try to change your body. You've probably tried multiple diets *and* multiple exercise plans. You could never add up all the minutes you've spent thinking about your body, being either frustrated or hopeful that you could change it. You've used resources, like money and relationships, to try to escape this curse that has haunted you for so long. Why, my friend, would you not apply some of that time and effort to fixing the one thing that's the key to all of it?

I'm going to detail the best process I know of for changing broken beliefs. Please, please, please follow my advice and do the work. Everything we've been talking about in this book, and all the things we still need to discuss before we're done here, are so very important for you to understand; you have to intimately know what you're doing to yourself in order to begin to change. But the change process—the work that we're now coming to—is as essential as the knowing. It won't do you any good to be able to observe your harmful beliefs if you don't use what you know to improve your life and your body.

I can assure you that change will not happen quickly. I promise you that you will feel like it isn't working sometimes. I know that you'll want to quit. But I guarantee that you can change, and when you do, you'll have accomplished something wonderful, something that infiltrates your life and seems to make everything a little better.

Mindfulness

As we proved through the Examining Body Image exercise, the vast majority of your stressors regarding your body are mental responses to the things you think you see in your world. Other people don't typically approach you to tell you that you aren't attractive. You've created standards in your own mind that you're not living up to, and you're imposing your own opinions of yourself on the people around you while, in reality, they're likely oblivious to your insecurities other than the fact that they can sense that you are insecure. You can sense that they sense that you're insecure, and you use that as affirmation that they think you're not attractive. In short, almost all of this is created in *your* head, not theirs.

Fixing this problem requires mindfulness. Mindfulness is basically the ability to see what is happening in your mind. To return to a previous example, when you walk into a room full of strangers, you may think, "I look terrible, and everyone is looking at me. Now they're all judging me, and I just want to run out of here." Yet you have no facts at all to back this up. Nothing happened that couldn't be interpreted in exactly the opposite fashion if you were more confident. Since nobody actually told you what she was thinking, there is no reason why you couldn't respond by thinking, "Look at all these people who are interested in me. I can't wait to get to know each of them." In fact, the very next person to enter this same room might think exactly that and, as usual, you will never know it.

You think thoughts like this, and will continue to do so, because this is what you've practiced. You have a well-myelinated pathway in your brain that tells you exactly how to proceed in situations like this. The only way out is to practice something new. To do so, you have to catch yourself in the middle of these thought processes.

What I'm proposing here is that you walk into that room, begin your well-practiced negative pattern, and then stop yourself in mid-thought, saying, "Wait a minute! What am I doing? There's no need for this self-torture. I don't know a damn thing about what these people are thinking, and I certainly don't have to assume the worst."

The moment you realize that what you're doing is nothing more than *thinking*, that is the moment of mindfulness. In that moment, you've recognized thoughts in your head as nothing more than what they truly are: thoughts. That split second of discovery—that mindfulness—is where the magic lies.

If this seems spiritual or hippy-dippy so far, please bear with me. I'm not a spiritual dude, and I promise that we aren't going to end up anywhere fluffy.

The act of catching yourself in these thought patterns is *very* hard. It's extremely easy to get caught up in the raging river of our thoughts. You can be ripped downstream and over a waterfall to be pummeled on the rocks of frustration and self-loathing while never realizing that it's possible to stand on the shore and watch your thoughts go by without being shoved around by them. For another example, imagine that you're sitting in your car at a stoplight when this happens:

"Did I remember to send that email to Laura today?" (Fairly innocuous thought.)

"I hope so. What did that look on her face mean in the last meeting?" (Assumptions are coming.)

"I don't think she likes me." (Assumptions have been made.)

"I don't really fit in at work." (Getting worse.)

"I wish I didn't need this job. I'm so unhappy. My life is not turning out the way I always hoped it would." (Aaaaand now you're stressed out.)

What the hell? You were just sitting at a stoplight! Nothing in the real world changed at all. Earth is still spinning exactly as it was before you thought about that email, but now you're upset based on nothing more than a thought pattern in your head.

We all have these kinds of thoughts, and we can all come to realize that they are *only* thoughts. There's no reason why you couldn't just keep enjoying the song on the radio, the sun shining, or fond memories of your 10th birthday party. Thoughts alone hold so much power over us.

Mindfulness can intervene.

<u>Becoming More Mindful</u>

The most solid and direct path to more mindfulness, in my experience, is through meditation.

Wait! Stop reaching for your bookmark. Let me explain.

As I said, I'm not a spiritual guy. I don't want to offend you if you are a spiritual person, but I am a scientist by nature, and I'm not interested in aligning my chakras or finding my center. What I am interested in is changing thought patterns, and meditation absolutely does this on a level that can be seen as physical changes in an fMRI. In one very cool study called "Mindfulness practice leads to increases in regional brain gray matter density," researchers concluded the following:

This study demonstrates longitudinal changes in brain gray matter concentration following an 8-week Mindfulness-Based Stress Reduction course compared with a control group. Hypothesized increases in gray matter concentration within the left hippocampus were confirmed. Exploratory whole brain analyses identified significant increases in gray matter concentration in the PCC (posterior cingulate cortex), TPJ (temporoparietal junction), and the cerebellum.

Translation: Meditation isn't just about trying to teach yourself to think differently; it literally rewires parts of your brain. Can you imagine how valuable this might be in dealing with your inner voice? We can actually learn to change those knee-jerk thoughts by changing the very pathways in our brains. That is amazing!

As I write this, meditation is a hot topic. A search for "meditation" using Google Scholar (Google's search tool for scholarly articles and research papers) turns up 763,000 hits in under a second. Everyone, from Fortune 100 corporations to the Pentagon, is using meditation for a variety of purposes. However, the weight-loss world isn't using it as effectively as it could be. I think this is another problem of perspective.

I don't usually prescribe meditation as a way to relax unless it's being used to help someone sleep. The meditation that I'm asking you to do will be more like the kind of exercise you do when you lift weights. In fact, you could literally look at it like you're doing reps and sets. It's focused and intense. It requires lots of practice to get it right and finally see some amazing results. And it almost always feels silly for a while.

Meditation for this purpose will be intensive. I have experimented with it for years, prescribing it to thousands of people, and I can say without hesitation that all meditation is beneficial to virtually everyone. However, knowing exactly what you're trying to do—

convincing your mind to comply with new beliefs—makes the process much more effective.

Stress management will be a nice little ancillary benefit of a consistent meditation practice, and reduced stress will almost always make the biochemical aspects of fat loss easier. But I believe the ability to remove desperation, frustration, self-sabotage, unhelpful emotions, and harmful unsubstantiated assumptions from your head will be far more valuable to you than any reduction in stress that you experience.

For us, meditation will be practice for catching ourselves thinking. If you don't currently possess the mindfulness to see what you're doing when you're beating the hell out of yourself, you'll always go along for the ride. At every opportunity, your inner voice will push you into that raging river, and you'll be swept downstream. Meditation will teach you, first, to swim for the shore and, finally, to not allow yourself to be pushed in at all.

Before you ever sit down to meditate, be sure you're prepared to feel awkward for a while. You're going to tell yourself that you're terrible at this, that you have better things to do, and that you just aren't cut out for this meditation stuff. Everyone starts there, so expect it and don't allow yourself to believe any of those negative thoughts. The benefits come when you put in the time, but there usually isn't anything dramatic happening in each meditation. You might experience an "aha" moment once or twice, but you'll be better off if you think only in terms of accumulated benefits.

Meditation is very much like exercise for your brain. When you do biceps curls with dumbbells, you don't expect to look down after one set and see the massive biceps you might envision as your end goal. You know that only consistently performing this exercise for months will produce results. It's exactly the same with meditation.

Don't look for a recognizable outcome in any single meditation session.

Intensive Meditation

Here's how it works.

1. Place a chair in a quiet spot. A more rigid chair, like the desk or kitchen-table variety, will be better than a squishy, upholstered chair that might be a little too comfortable and potentially lull you to sleep. If you don't have a perfectly quiet place to meditate and you need some comforting ambient noise, you can use a smartphone meditation app like Calm.
2. Sit with good posture, both feet on the floor, and your hands resting in your lap. Try to stay in good posture throughout your meditation session. You should be upright and awake, but not overly tense.
3. Take a couple of deep breaths, set a timer or meditation app for three minutes (for your first time), and close your eyes.
4. Try to breathe naturally. Focus on wherever you feel your breath the most. If you feel it at the tip of your nose, then that will be where you will focus your mind throughout your session. If you feel your breath in your chest, then focus there.
5. Once you've found your focal point, try to quiet your mind and think of nothing else except your breath.
6. Your mind *will* wander. Random thoughts *will* sneak back into your mind. You aren't doing anything wrong, and you aren't a bad meditator. Simply return to your focal point as soon as you realize that you've lost your focus. Do your best to return to your focal point without any additional internal commentary. There is no need to think, "You big dummy! Your mind is wandering again!" Just go back to breathing.
7. Repeat this pattern until your timer goes off.
8. Take a couple of deep breaths and continue on with your day.

Begin with just three minutes a day until you feel comfortable with that duration. There's no need to rush the process or force yourself into anything too uncomfortable. Taking on more than you can handle will only make it more likely that you'll get frustrated and quit. Keep your expectations low and just do it. After a week or two of three-minute sessions, go up to four minutes. Then five minutes. Many people will see excellent benefits after a few weeks of just five minutes of meditation per day.

When five minutes a day is comfortable for you, I recommend that you try increasing to ten minutes for a week or two to see if you reap even more benefits. Some people have a hard time getting into a meditation groove in just five minutes, while others have no problem. Personally, I never meditate for longer than ten minutes, but you're welcome to experiment.

Meditating at the same time each day can make it much easier to stick it out over the long haul, but fitting it in wherever you can each day is fine, too. Consistency is key, meaning that you need to meditate every day, but it isn't absolutely essential that you do it on a schedule.

And Then It Happens

One day soon, you'll stumble on proof that meditation is working for you. My own experience was awesome. I was cruising along, business as usual, when I started stressing about the potential outcome of a project I was working on. I wasn't even done with the project yet, but I was worrying that it wouldn't be as well-accepted by my online following as I hoped. Then, from left field, the realization that I was only thinking popped into my head. Nothing had happened. I was just suffering at the hands of random thoughts and an inner voice that wanted me to feel bad. I thought, "What am I doing? This isn't necessary, and it certainly isn't helping." I took a couple of deep breaths, focusing on each one like I would in a meditation session, and I was fully back in control. For the rest of the day, I kept returning to that moment and feeling like I had gained a superpower. I couldn't help but look around at everyone else I saw and think, "You're all suffering needlessly!"

I've heard from so many people with similar stories. Here's an email from a client who would like to remain anonymous:

I was out walking and thinking about my body and how mad it makes me. I had seen some great results, but I saw pictures of someone who was getting much faster results than I was, and I guess I was having an impatient moment. I actually stopped walking and said out loud, 'Stop it! You're being crazy! Everything is working!' I felt great the rest of the day. I would never have figured any of this out if you hadn't kept telling us to meditate until I finally gave in. Thank you!

It's truly a magical thing when your inner voice begins to lose its sway over you. When you can see your thoughts for what they are, you gain the ability to choose a different from than the ones that hurt. But you *must* put in the work. If I've done my job in this chapter, working on your body without putting at least as much effort into fixing your head will feel frivolous and nonsensical to you from now on. How can you hope to successfully change your body if the head that drives it is busy wrestling with itself?

<u>Where Do the Emotions Go?</u>

In one episode of my podcast, I happened to be beating the meditation drum particularly hard when my co-host, Erica, brought up a valid point. We were talking about a post in our forums in which the poster said a lot of things like, "I was feeling pretty much like…" and "I started feeling sorry for myself…" and "I was feeling bad…" and "Crawling into a hole of self-pity and self-loathing…." My response was that if she were to take all the emotion out, there wouldn't be much left in that post. I asked, "What would lifestyle change be like without the emotion? Do the emotions add anything necessary or beneficial?"

Erica replied, "I actually had a conversation about that post and your response. You're right. We, especially women, put emotion behind everything. It's just logic that's left when we take the emotions out, but we still *have* those emotions. We're still feeling those feelings. So, when you take them out, what do you do with them? Is that the purpose of meditation, to say, 'Those things don't make sense'?"

It might seem like I'm suggesting that you use meditation to fight against your emotions for the rest of your life, but that's not really my point. The results of a successful meditation practice, when used as I'm recommending it here, will unfold like this:

1. You'll recognize your negative thoughts while they're happening. "Oh, no, everyone is looking at me, and I look terrible. I wish I wasn't.... Wait a damn minute! What am I doing? I have no idea what those people are thinking. I don't have to beat myself up like this! Take a deep breath or two and get on with being awesome."
2. You eventually get to a place where you catch yourself more often than you don't. The practice is paying off, and your purposeful reframing of these situations is becoming your new normal.
3. With enough time and consistency, you begin to skip the self-loathing thoughts altogether, jumping straight to the part that used to require purposeful intervention. "Everyone is looking at me. How nice that they're interested in who I am. I should make some new friends today."

I'm not telling you to live in denial. If you still have the negative emotions, then you still have work to do. As much as those emotions might seem like part of who you are, there are plenty of people in the world who don't have those same emotions in those same situations. Since your emotions aren't a ubiquitous human trait that everyone has, they are subjective. *Subjective* usually means there is a choice involved, or at least a potential for change. You can become one of those people who would not feel the same way you do. Sure, it will always be hard to change these things that run so deep in your personal psychology, but change *is* possible. The sequence I just described might take more than a year, but isn't the alternative—many more years of getting your ass kicked by your inner voice—so much worse?

I'll Beg if I Must

If you're still on the fence about meditation, please do me a personal favor and try it for a month. I've been coaching fat loss for a long time, and I have never been surer of anything that I prescribe. Bodies react to different stimuli in different ways, but I have yet to meet anyone who didn't see her life improve with a consistent meditation practice.

Please. Just give meditation an honest shot. I want you to succeed.

Chapter Thirty-Three
Willpower

AT SOME POINT, you've likely said, "I don't have any will-power when it comes to _____." Maybe it is a particular confection, like cheesecake, that you "just can't resist." While it's true that we all have certain things that tempt us more than others, we don't have contextual willpower. In reality, we all have one pool of willpower, and it's an exhaustible supply.

Kelly McGonigal, in her must-read book *The Willpower Instinct*, explains this limited resource like this:

Welcome to one of the most robust, if troubling, findings from the science of self-control: People who use their willpower seem to run out of it. Smokers who go without a cigarette for twenty-four hours are more likely to binge on ice cream. Drinkers who resist their favorite cocktail become physically weaker on a test of endurance. Perhaps most disturbing, people who are on a diet are more likely to cheat on their spouse. It's as if there's only so much willpower to go around. Once exhausted, you are left defenseless against temptation—or at least disadvantaged.

Researchers are largely in agreement that willpower is much like a muscle in that it is fatigable. You start your day with a limited supply and then dip into it each time life requires you to choose the harder thing when the easier thing calls out to you.

Willpower is manufactured in the prefrontal cortex, a recent evolutionary development in our brains. We have the most advanced prefrontal cortex in the animal kingdom, with other social animals, like primates, following behind us. When you live in social groups that provide a lot of benefit to each individual, willpower is a necessary function of the brain. If you cram down as much food as you can get into your face without sharing, then eventually people will stop sharing with you. If you have a bad day hunting and take it out on everyone back at camp, then you should expect to eventually alienate the people who help keep you alive on those unsuccessful days. Willpower is what we use to resist reacting upon every little emotional impulse that would make our survival harder.

Unfortunately, life in modern society demands that we use willpower for all kinds of things that our hunter-gatherer ancestors did not deal with. For example, your day might look like this:

- You get up to an alarm clock when staying in bed would be wonderful.
- You force yourself to get ready for work, choosing the right clothes and grooming yourself in ways that you wouldn't have to if you were able to stay home and chill on the couch.
- You eat a healthy breakfast instead of stopping at McDonald's for an Egg McMuffin.
- You go to a job that you would never return to if you didn't need money.
- You do work that is not fun and doesn't actually feed any of your innate drives the way hunting and gathering would.
- You narrowly avoid eating one of the donuts in the breakroom.
- You're nice to people whom you would rather not have to work with.

- You refrain from telling your boss that he's a complete ass and that an untrained monkey could do a better job of motivating people than he does.
- You make healthy food choices at lunch while your friends eat highly palatable crap in front of you.
- On the way home, someone cuts you off in traffic and you stop yourself from flipping him off because he has a kid in his car (and, of course, because you're a good person).
- You stop at the grocery store and buy healthy food to cook for dinner instead of ordering a pizza and putting your tired feet up.
- When you get home, your partner and kids are preoccupied with various things and don't seem happy to see you, but you manage to keep yourself from wringing their ungrateful little necks after the hard day you put yourself through for them.

After all of these self-control-depleting events, you remember that there's half a carton of ice cream in the freezer, and you don't have a drop of willpower left in the tank. You succumb, you're rewarded for 30 seconds or so, and then you feel bad about your decision. One more negative event has now been piled on top of an un-awesome day of doing things you would rather have skipped.

With meditation in place, you'll gain the ability to catch yourself in those moments of weakness and avoid temptation to do something you'll regret. However, you also need to game your use of willpower to the best of your ability. With this understanding of willpower and how it works, you can try to keep some in reserve so you can make it to the end of your day without running out.

Sleep is a huge factor here. Multiple studies have shown that if your sleep patterns suck, you'll have less willpower. More to our example, though, if you go to bed earlier, you might need less willpower to get out of bed when your alarm clock goes off. Many of the other factors of your day are not going to be in your control, like your jerk of a boss, but maybe you can avoid the break room entirely, rather than staring at those donuts and fighting your primal desire to eat one or five.

The rest of your day aside, nothing will be more important than doing everything you can to make your home a place where willpower (in regards to your fat-loss goals) is not necessary. That ice cream in the freezer has to go. You can't depend on willpower to keep you away from it. It takes a lot less mindfulness to intervene on temptation when you would have to get in your car and drive somewhere in order to get your drug of choice. Standing up and walking to the kitchen, on the other hand, can happen so fast that you're basically helpless to resist. You could find yourself staring at the bottom of an empty bowl before you're even present enough to really think about what you're doing.

In short, you need to give your limited supply of willpower all the support you can possibly offer. You aren't weak; the cards are just stacked against you, once again, by this wacky modern world where all the rules have been changed. Don't ever let this fact slip your mind. Putting yourself in situations in which you are forced to white-knuckle your way through temptation is a recipe for failure, regret, and guilt. Take control and, whenever possible, don't depend on willpower alone.

Chapter Thirty-Four
Live the Way You Want to Look

AS YOU KNOW, I didn't write this book to tell you how to physically go through the process of losing weight. What we're doing here is examining and, hopefully, changing the beliefs and perspectives that keep you from success.

However, we need to talk about a subject that falls in the gray area between those two poles. That subject is the belief that most people have regarding what fat loss, the physical part, really is. I've been dropping hints since we started this ride together, but now I'm going to put a fine point on it and remove any chance of confusion on your part.

Think about the last time you saw a physically fit woman who you believed was over 35 years of age. I'm not talking about someone who was just small, shaped particularly well with her curves in the right place, high cheekbones, and good hair. I'm talking about real health and vitality—the kind that is undeniable and stands out. The kind that makes you stop and think, "Wow, she glows with vitality and carries herself like she loves life!" Not a super-common sight, but I'm sure you can remember someone like that if you try.

When you saw this woman, you probably thought, "She's so lucky that all those amazing things happened to her by accident through no effort on her part." Right? Of course not!

You inherently understand that you're seeing someone who has worked for what she has. There might be some good genetics there, but you'd be shocked to see her shotgunning beers and eating pizza like a frat boy after finals.

Youth can produce beauty by accident, but we always suspect that we're seeing something temporary. If you're older than 35, you're less likely to wish that you looked like the pretty 20-year-old than you are to just wish you were young again. If you are 20 and comparing yourself with someone you think is beautiful, it's a different story, but you have already seen some of the prettiest girls from your high school completely fall apart. The luck factor is still quite real.

Exercise fanaticism can produce pleasing body shapes, but the oxidative stress caused by not being able to pry yourself out of the gym almost always produces premature aging that is very apparent well before middle age. Sometimes these women will have nice muscle tone and a good shape, but they often have traded their youthful skin and hair, and sometimes their reproductive health (depending on their exercise methods), for their gains in the gym. More often, though, the exercise addicted end up sinewy, overly lean, imbalanced, or just small and squishy. For an example of this, picture your friend who's addicted to running. She's probably relatively thin, but she also probably doesn't have any glutes (butt muscles) to speak of, and she's not firm and well-toned.

In a world where very few people are truly fit, it can be easy to allow yourself to believe that the opposite of fat is skinny. I beg to differ. The opposite of fat is healthy.

Broken-record time again: Sustainable fat loss happens through improved health.

That truly beautiful and vital woman I asked you to recall a moment ago stands out, even among the young or overtrained, because she has what we all recognize as true beauty—health and vitality.

Why am I telling you all this in a book about fat-loss psychology? So that I can ask you these two questions:

1.   Are you healthy and vital right now?
2.   Should you be?

If you spend a lot of your day sitting, if your diet looks like a perpetual pursuit of flavor, if sleep is a burden, and/or if chronic stress is just a part of your life that you've come to accept, which part of all that are you expecting to produce health? Is it the new cleanse you just read about on Pinterest? Or the new boot camp you just signed up for? Maybe the problem is just food in general and starvation is your answer. Do you honestly believe that peak health happens through those means?

When I said before that fat loss is all about adaptation, I promised you an explanation. Well, this is it. Just like with our minds, our bodies become what we practice. If you treat your body like you love it, while simultaneously asking it to do the things it evolved to do on a regular basis, you will mold yourself into a remarkable human specimen. Punishing your body with starvation and a constant barrage of workouts that simulate emergencies will only make your body think that life on earth sucks and that it should adapt however possible to keep you alive, usually by hoarding fat wherever it can. Likewise, if you adapt your body to this modern world where palatability is king, nutrition is an afterthought, and movement has been almost entirely outsourced, then you will get the incapable, unhealthy, unattractive body that you asked for.

Unless you've suffered a major disease or debilitating disorder that was not in any way related to your lifestyle choices, you currently have a body that's a product of the way you live. If you want a different body, you have no choice but to live the way you want to look. Evolution will always get a say in this process, and there are no shortcuts. The belief that there's a trick that you haven't yet tried or a gimmick that you haven't yet purchased that will make you beautiful is a belief that ends in disappointment.

I know this isn't easy to hear, but these are the facts. Please understand that I'm not saying, "Your current condition is entirely your fault, and you should be ashamed of yourself!" You've been repeatedly misled, and none of us are supposed to have to think about any of these things at all. Remember, the default product of living in nature was health (aside from a greater potential for infectious disease and injury), but that's no longer the case. My point is that you should not try or expect anything that doesn't sound 100 percent rational from here forward. You're now educated, at least on the basic concept of what fat loss really is, and you now know that when you live a healthy lifestyle, not one that employs desperate torture, for an extended period of time you will be successful.

There's one more thing about adaptation that needs to be included in your beliefs before we move on, and this one might help explain many of your past frustrations. Adaptation, by definition, means to become adjusted to new conditions. Notice that the definition is not "to become adjusted to something that just happened for a minute." Nor is it "to become adjusted to something that occasionally happens." The word "conditions" implies stimuli that are ongoing and constant.

Let's use Pavlov's dogs as an example. In case you aren't familiar with Ivan Pavlov and his famous conditioning experiments, I'll break them down for you. The short version is that Pavlov always sounded an audible cue (like a buzzer) before feeding his canine subjects. After a while, the dogs would salivate whenever they heard the sound, even if food was not present.

Only consistency over an extended period of time created the adaptation (conditioning) that Pavlov was looking for. If he had sounded the buzzer and fed his dogs two days in a row, and then randomly sounded the buzzer for another two days without also feeding his dogs, Pavlov would have had a hard time convincing them that anything should be associated with the buzzer.

I'm creating a rather simplistic example here, but you can look at the adaptation required for weight loss as roughly the same as what Pavlov did in his experiments. You're trying to convince your body that life is awesome and it does not need to store a lot of excess fat. You're teaching it that it can depend on a regular supply of healthy food without a bunch of garbage that it doesn't understand. And you're helping it to understand that sleep, stress, and exercise will all come in doses it can manage without freaking out. All of that convincing will require consistency.

The difference between Pavlov's conditioning protocol and that of the average fat-loss trick is that Pavlov never thought of his buzzer as a magical way to make dogs salivate. When most people try to lose fat, they aren't considering the adaptation involved; they're simply applying some strange stimulus, like removing a specific number of calories or one macronutrient and jumping on the scale every day to see if it's "working." If someone stumbles on a protocol that could actually get her healthy and fit, she will tend to bring that same "dieting" mentality to the table, and adaptation is still ignored. We see this in people who exclaim, "I was doing it 80 percent of the time! Why didn't I get 80 percent of the results?"

My good friend and fellow fat-loss coach Mark Rogers uses a fantastic analogy. He says that adapting your body to a new, healthy lifestyle is a lot like pedaling hard to get your bike up a hill. Each time you think, "One slice of cake won't hurt," it's like you stopped pedaling for a minute, and you start to roll back down the hill. While it is true that one slice of cake never made anyone fat, eating cake while you're trying to convince your body of a new *normal* way of eating will be just like Pavlov sounding his buzzer without feeding his dogs—only confusion can come of it. When you get to the top of the hill, then you'll be able to coast. Your new lifestyle will be well-ingrained and habitual. Then, and only then, will the occasional piece of cake be seen by your body as a random oddity rather than making it think, "Cake! I remember this! We must be heading back down the hill to our familiar way of eating!"

As I said, I'm simplifying things a lot, and what we're really accomplishing are much more scientific things like improved metabolic flexibility and metabolic rate, but these analogies get the job done when what we're addressing here is your belief about how weight loss should unfold.

Partial efforts will occasionally impart partial results, but you shouldn't expect them. Adaptation means becoming something new for long enough for your body to recognize the new way as normal and the old way as abandoned. Once again, we've shut down the proposed logic of weight-loss tricks. You have to stop looking for shortcuts and get down to the business of adaptation.

Change your thinking for long enough to change your lifestyle for long enough to change your body forever.

Chapter Thirty-Five
A New Metric

YOU MAY STILL be processing some of the concepts I've been throwing at you, but we need to jump ahead and assume that you've accepted a couple of them. When you believe that 1) we must get healthy to achieve sustainable weight loss and 2) getting healthy requires adaptation to a healthier lifestyle, then the "smaller at any cost" mentality must go out the window.

It's always so sad when I hear a woman say something like, "I had the flu last week. It was horrible. I couldn't get out of bed. But I lost eight pounds, so there was an upside." When did *smaller* become the holy grail?

With health as your focus, muscle must be preserved. To my current knowledge, there is nothing more strongly correlated to health and vitality than muscle mass. Peak health equals a capable body. And peak health equals an attractive body.

Why the review? Because simply driving down the number on your scale is not specific enough. Your scale measures gravity's effect on you, and reducing that effect only requires a loss of matter. Obviously, if you lost a limb, you would weigh less, but you don't go looking for a saw when you want to be more attractive.

I've used the terms "weight loss" and "fat loss" interchangeably so far, but in reality nobody should ever have a *weight-loss* goal. Losing weight (fat and muscle) will *never* leave a body as attractive as losing only fat.

I'm absolutely positive that this concept will be one of the hardest sells of this whole book. But I have to try. Allow me to at least propose something shocking. I can't come to your home and force anything upon you, but hear me out. Okay, here we go! Wait for it…

Maybe you don't need to know what you weigh.

"Preposterous! Insanity!" Maybe, but what are you actually achieving when you weigh yourself? What do you learn about your body that truly correlates to your physical appearance? Human eyes are incapable of calculating the weight of the objects they view. We can't *see* weight. What we *can* see is shape. So don't circumference measurements make a lot more sense?

If you are currently in a relationship, think back to when your partner met you and was smitten. He was thinking about you all day and longed to be with you when you were apart. But did he know how much you weighed at the time?

How much does your car weigh? If you don't know, then how do you know if it's a good-looking car?

When you see an attractive man, are you unsure about exactly how attractive he is until you know how much he weighs?

If you see an attractive woman and then find out she's heavier than you would have thought she was, does she instantly become less attractive? Do you think you could run up to any man who might be admiring her and tell him how much she really weighs and watch him walk away in disappointment?

I'm being a bit facetious again, but this is important because I honestly believe that the world would be a very different place for women if weight had never become the metric by which you assess attraction in yourselves. Sadly, you are focused on a metric that's not telling you what you really want to know, but it often becomes an obstacle by allowing you to lose some of the health that would improve attraction, all while you convince yourself that you're winning. You are very privately saying to yourself, "I want to be better-looking, so I'll judge my aesthetics (literally defined visually) by measuring how hard I press down on the earth." It's madness!

I don't love the idea of any woman constantly measuring anything about herself, but if you must have a metric, make it one that we can at least see. Measure your waist, hips, chest, whatever, and you'll be assessing something much more logical. More importantly, when you measure yourself with a tape instead of a scale, you should be much less tempted to do anything silly.

In my private Facebook group, we saw so many people posting things like, "I've lost only a pound in three weeks. Am I doing something wrong?" Other group members would ask, "What happened to your measurements?" The original poster would reply, "Since you asked, I just measured myself, and I'm down three inches in my waist! How is that possible?" Eventually, we had to make it a rule that members are not allowed to post any change in their weight without also posting measurement changes. This nips the whole thing in the bud and lets everyone know that I'm serious about the uselessness of the scale. If they insist on staying in their dysfunctional relationship with their scale, they'll have to do it elsewhere.

I have worked with many women who wore size 6 jeans, and among them I have seen a range of at least 30 pounds at the same height. When I looked at them with my human eyes, I saw a body that fit into size 6 jeans. That's all. However, the women on the heavier end of that spectrum almost always had more muscle, which also means they were carrying less body fat and they were more likely to be comfortable in a bikini. If those same women were hung up on their weight, they would have been actively trying to become less attractive by losing some of the muscle tone that gave them their curves and overall aesthetic appeal—all because they were letting gravity be the final judge.

It might come as a shock to some people, but we can live without knowing what we weigh. Throwing your scale in a dumpster will not cause you to wither and die. No autopsy ever reported "scale deprivation" as the cause of death.

There's so much heartache wrapped up in our modern need to know what we weigh. Can you think of a time in your adult life when you didn't know *exactly* what you weighed? Probably not. You can be free of this without giving up on fat loss. True fat loss can be measured by a tape measure or by the fit of your clothes.

I have clients who could tell you that I made them bring me their bathroom scales before I would work with them. Sometimes it just isn't possible for me to get someone to a healthy mental state with that damn thing calling to them all the time.

I don't expect you to beat a scale addiction by simply reading this chapter (that would be cool, though), but I hope you will give it some thought. Bathroom scales aren't so expensive that throwing yours out would have to be a permanent decision. You could always buy another one. Although, if you do get rid of it for long enough to begin to think differently about weight as opposed to shape, I'll bet my bottom dollar that you'll be happier.

Chapter Thirty-Six
Trends Trump Snapshots

IN A WORLD where diet and exercise programs regularly make promises about how much you'll lose in a specified amount of time, it can be easy to assume that weight loss should happen in a linear, predictable fashion. Nothing could be further from the truth.

Throughout my career I have helped to create a lot of astonishing transformations—the kind where someone loses a substantial amount of fat and keeps it off for long enough that people stop wondering when she'll gain it all back. In all of those cases, not once have I seen someone lose fat in the same increments per week or month. Nobody has ever lost a pound a week, or 10 pounds a month, or any other consistent number of pounds over any unit of time. In fact, the one thing that is always predictable is that fat loss will not happen in a predictable fashion.

When a diet promises that a specific amount of fat or weight will be lost each week, I know I don't have to look any further—this one is just another scam. Our bodies don't work that way, and they never will.

This is another very important concept for you to remember, because forgetting it will leave you vulnerable to the kind of disappointment that can derail you. You need realistic expectations, not impossible ideals.

A realistic example of 10 pounds of sustainable fat loss might look like this:

Week 1: Down 3 pounds
Week 2: Down 2 pounds
Week 3: Down 1 pound
Week 4: Up 2 pounds
Week 5: No loss or gain
Week 6: Down 2 pounds
Week 7: Down 2 pounds
Week 8: Down 1 pound
Week 9: No loss or gain
Week 10: Down 1 pound

If this is you, will you quit at Week 4? Most people do.

We can stretch this example out over much more time, too. My wife, Sheryl, has gone from a size 18 to a size 6, but the process was anything but linear. At times, she went whole months without a single change in any measurement, only to see noticeable changes again in the following two weeks.

Here's another hypothetical example for you. Let's say you have 40 pounds to lose, and you've lost and regained at least 20 of those pounds half a dozen times in the past decade. At this point, you find something that could really work, something that could give you the sustainable fat loss you've always wanted. Unfortunately, you bring all your past experience to the table, including all the expectations and ideals that have been drilled into your head.

In the beginning, you see some rapid results, losing eight pounds in just three weeks. Then the number on the scale stops moving and doesn't budge for two terribly frustrating weeks. During that time, though, your sleep improves, your skin seems softer, you feel less bloated, and your sex drive revs up. Since all your other fat-loss endeavors were aimed solely at weighing less and not at getting healthier, you ignore all of these awesome little victories and begin weighing yourself more often, telling yourself that nothing is happening.

At around the three-week mark of no new changes on the scale, you decide it's time to throw in the towel. Through the magic of fictional examples, however, we can see the future and know that it was going to be another three weeks before fat loss started again. Then, after losing another ten pounds in seven weeks, you were going to stop losing weight again for another two months. Then lose again and stop, repeating this totally unpredictable process until you reached your goal in a total of eleven months.

"Eleven *months?*!" you cry. Yes, sometimes it can take quite a while to repair a complex and unique human body, especially if past choices have conditioned your body to hold onto fat for dear life. The real problem here is not that your body is unrepairable, but that your head is laying down ground rules for how everything must unfold in order for you to stay diligent. Your beliefs are actually more broken than your body. Toss some desperation and body loathing into the mix, and you have a bunch of insurmountable obstacles in your path, all of which live only inside your head.

If your beliefs about the process of fat loss were forged in the fires of the often-ridiculous weight-loss industry, then your expectations might be just as broken as the industry itself. Snapshots are worthless. Trends are everything.

In my professional opinion, plateaus don't happen in less than three months. In other words, you can't say that you're stuck and results aren't coming anymore unless you've been holding a steady lifestyle pattern for at least three months without seeing any benefit to your health. Please note the "any benefit to your health" part. If you're seeing improvements to things like digestion, sleep patterns, mood, sex drive, skin, hair, or any physical disorder, then you're still moving in the right direction, even if fat loss has paused. Remember, peak health is the goal. Therefore, any improvement to health is a step toward the fat-loss finish line.

Use this information to keep from getting frustrated and quitting. A person who truly understands this concept is someone who will not weigh and measure herself frequently. She understands the futility of watching her body like a hawk and using the fluctuations of her weight and measurements to draw any kind of conclusion in the short term. I know this is a huge departure from the norm, especially when some of the biggest weight-loss companies will literally weigh you every week and then try to alter their advice according to what their scales say, but I need you to trust me on this.

We aren't wired for long views, but nothing else will work here. If you have 20 or 30 pounds to lose and you weigh yourself even weekly, I can almost assure you that you'll encounter at least a week or two in which you either don't lose any fat or you actually gain a pound or two. We'll talk about one reason for this in the next chapter, but my point is that you need to try to think of your fat-loss journey in months and years rather than days and weeks.

Assess your progress no more than once a week—less often would actually be better—and then take each individual assessment with a grain of salt. When you have at least a couple of months of data to look at, you will begin to see the real picture of your progress. If any one assessment gets you down, you know what to do. (Hint: It starts with an "M" and ends with "editate.")

Chapter Thirty-Seven
Cycles and Hormones and Fat Loss, Oh, My!

IF YOU ARE past menarche and before menopause, it is a simple fact that you have no two days in your cycle in which your steroidal hormones are at identical levels. To say this another way, if you currently have a menstrual cycle, the combination of estrogen, testosterone, and progesterone in your body is never exactly the same as any other day in your 28-day cycle. I believe it goes without saying that these hormones have a dramatic effect on lots of things in your body, and fat loss is no exception.

Between menstruation and ovulation (the follicular phase), estrogen and testosterone will reach their peaks and progesterone will be lower. Between ovulation and menstruation (the luteal phase), progesterone will reach its peak while estrogen and testosterone ebb.

During the follicular phase, with estrogen and testosterone on the rise, fat loss will be easier if all other variables are the same. However, the psychological effect that these hormones impart (mood, confidence, etc.) should not be ignored. During her follicular phase, if you tell your 16-year-old daughter that her pants are too tight, she'll probably shrug off your comment like you're too old and uncool to know what you're talking about. Make the same comment in her luteal phase, and she might react as if you've just said, "You're fat and everyone hates you." Of course that's an extreme example, but with this influence that these hormones potentially exert on the psychology of the average woman, I would venture to guess that more women quit diets during the luteal phase of their cycles than during the follicular phase (but I'm only speculating).

I'm telling you all this to further illustrate the fact that trends trump snapshots, but also to remind you that you need to cut yourself some slack sometimes. Realistic expectations, along with the compassion to be nice to yourself on those days when the odds are stacked against you, are essential if you want to succeed. Here again you can see why weighing yourself even as often as once a week could produce frustrating results, but it's also important to note that the likelihood of fat loss stalling or reversing is also higher at the same time that you might be less capable of taking it in stride.

All these hormone fluctuations are normal. In fact, they are a lot more natural than dieting will ever be. You will remember that premodern women didn't deal with any of this wacky dieting stuff, but menstrual cycles are quite literally why any of us are here to begin with. What isn't normal is the belief that hormone fluctuations don't matter to your goals. They do matter. A lot.

As a side note, I have no love for hormonal methods of birth control. I need to make it clear that I am not a doctor and what follows is only my opinion.

As a form of life on planet earth, we have three basic jobs: find some food, try not to die, and breed. The first two are totally subservient to the last one. Some of us choose not to breed, but most of us pass our genetics downstream. Regardless of what we choose or don't choose, procreation is part of the definition of life, and your body is very much geared toward that end. Messing with the system on a chemical level is like altering one of the fundamental aspects of what it means to be alive at a foundational level. In my opinion—and please acknowledge that "opinion" word—mechanical forms of birth control will always be better options. That's all I will say on that subject.

Acknowledge your cycle and the hormonal changes it brings. You are a woman. Women are awesome. Be nice to yourself.

Chapter Thirty-Eight
Disorders and Physical Obstacles

LET ME PREFACE this chapter by once again pointing out that I am not a doctor, and I can't give you medical advice. If you have any kind of symptom that might point to something debilitating or life-threatening, you absolutely need to seek medical attention. I can, however, try to give you a new perspective on some of the things that many experts will want to treat you for.

We live in a world where nearly everyone can be diagnosed with *something*. From adrenal fatigue to all manner of gut dysbiosis to hypothyroidism to systemic inflammation to fibromyalgia—if you've been living a less-than-stellar lifestyle, then someone can find something wrong with you that could be treated.

I will argue, though, that nobody should want treatment of any kind. Yes, sometimes it's necessary, but I believe that it should be a last resort. My reason for believing this is that I've seen more disorders than I can name vanish entirely or dramatically improve when people simply gave their bodies everything they needed to get healthy again. There are plenty of people who will argue with me on this, but I can't ignore my anecdotal experience.

Sadly, there's a trend right now in which people are seeking out experts online who are all too willing to order a few tests and then prescribe supplements at exorbitant prices to treat whatever they find without ever trying to correct the lifestyle patterns that may have caused the problems and are certainly inhibiting the correction of them.

What I'm saying is that if you have something like adrenal fatigue, for example, you will have no problem finding someone to prescribe a treatment for your disorder, but if you did everything you could to get as healthy as possible, you just might heal by accident along the way.

You could be spending a lot of money that you don't need to spend, but the part that worries me is actually much worse. If you've spent your adult life struggling with your weight, a diagnosis from an expert can give you something to blame. Once you know you have a disorder and you're taking something to "fix" it, your chances of real success might go out the window. It sounds like this: "I've only been doing 50 percent of what I know I need to do to get healthy, but the real reason I'm not getting results is that I have _____!" It's a convenient and comfortable way to let yourself off the hook after so much frustration.

Lifestyle change is hard. Blaming a disorder for your problems and then popping pills without ever finding out what your body might be capable of if it was given what it needs is not hard at all.

I have watched so many women fall by the wayside after someone told them they had a disorder. It saddens me, but I can see the subconscious appeal of believing that you don't have to make so many changes anymore. If you ever seek treatment for anything that could be related to your lifestyle choices, you can't let yourself fall into the trap of believing that you've discovered the thing that was wrong all along. You still have to get as healthy as possible if you want to win. Removing most disorders will not magically give you a beautiful, healthy body, so what's the point in believing that you have just been a victim this whole time and success was never within your grasp anyway?

Stay the course. Get as healthy as you can, and then see what's left. You may still need some help, but don't fall prey to these people who just want to part you from your money and give you an excuse to fail.

Chapter Thirty-Nine
More Is Not Better

IN THE WESTERN world, we have some odd beliefs about how hard things should be and how results should always improve with more of any stimulus.

Yoga wasn't good enough until we added heat and power to it.

You only run a couple of miles a week? Well, that woman over there ran four marathons last year.

Marathons? Those are for people who are too weak to run ultramarathons.

We even do it with sleep. When someone says he only slept five hours last night, there's sometimes a hint of bragging in the implication that he has too much going on to be troubled with sleeping eight hours a night.

Similarly, we often assume that when something is working, or when we believe something will work, the proper thing to do is double our efforts. Unfortunately, that's usually not the way things work when your goal is to create health and fat loss. In fact, almost everything that you must do to get healthy can easily be taken to an extreme that will halt progress and detract from health, even when those things don't feel so extreme to your Western-world brain.

For example, a small reduction in calories will likely produce health benefits for many people who aren't already starving themselves, but extreme reductions in calories break metabolisms and make people fatter in the end.

Things get even trickier with exercise. The reality is that nobody has ever made a gain of any kind *in* any workout. Exercise is the stimulus that creates results *during recovery*. In other words, when you go to the gym, you apply acute stressors to your body that cause it to become stronger, leaner, and healthier *after* it has recovered from those stressors. This fact is clearly misunderstood by everyone who works out six or seven days a week.

This "more is better" mentality can be applied to almost anything. Many times I have seen people try to alter a perfectly good fat-loss plan by increasing the difficulty of the guidelines. They think, "If I should be reducing processed carbs to get good results, then I'll just remove *all* carbs and get great results!" Or, "If I should be cycling my calorie intake, then I'll just not eat at all on some days!" Or, "If walking is good for me, then running must be fantastic!"

This desire to smash the gas pedal to the floor and race through fat loss like a bat out of hell must be quelled. Whether it's driven by desperation or a need to prove something to yourself, this belief is almost always destructive.

More is always better when we are talking about healthy lifestyle changes that you have not yet started, but once you have applied these changes to your life, the line where more becomes *not* better is likely closer than you think.

It's okay to be a minimalist. It's okay—better even—to do your best to apply just the right amount of stimulus to achieve your goals without becoming a diet and exercise hobbyist. Sometimes it can be hard to not get sucked in by the allure of a fun new lifestyle change, such as exercising with a group of people you like, but you will regret it if you lose sight of your true goals. Don't get me wrong. Almost anything that is overdone will produce results for a while, but every change you make must be sustainable. Don't let your inner voice persuade you to ruin something good.

Chapter Forty
The Allure of Big Goals

BIG GOALS ARE exciting! When you set one, it's all you can think about for a while. In fact, setting a new goal has some appeal that is independent of actually achieving it, because of the escape it can provide from your self-torment.

In a fantastic research paper titled "The False-Hope Syndrome: Unfulfilled Expectations of Self-Change," there are some thought-provoking ideas that might hit close to home. For example, we can start with this quote:

Merely committing to a diet may make people feel more in control, more responsible for their weight, and, potentially, more likely to achieve their goals than they felt before making the commitment.

This is certainly good news, but there's more to the story:

Unfortunately, however, the optimism and positive affect that accompany the beginning of a change attempt tend to dissipate with the vicissitudes of actually working to effect the change.

In other words, it feels awesome to set a new goal, but we often harbor overinflated expectations of the outcome, leading to a hard fall when the real work begins. Nonetheless, the goal-setting part still feels great.

This should sound familiar to everyone. When are you most likely to set a new goal to change your body? That's an easy one: You really want change when you are at a low point and most dissatisfied with yourself. While looking in the mirror and listening intently to every little insult your inner voice is spewing at you, you put your foot down and vow to change yourself—once and for all.

What happens then is amazing! From that point forward, you feel happy, strong, empowered, and valuable, and all without doing anything except *deciding* to make this change that is important to you. For at least a short time, you have escaped that horrible inner voice by identifying with what you will become. No doubt about it: The day you set a new goal is always a good day.

Then it happens: the bitter realization that the goal-setting part was the part that feels the best, and everything else is hard work. Proclaiming your intention to change put you on cloud nine, but actually *doing* the changing is serious business and requires a heap of dedication. To make matters worse, you set a huge goal—because the bigger the goal, the better it feels when you set it—and you have all but doomed yourself to failure, which means your inner voice is warming up to rain hell down upon you.

I firmly believe that success can be much easier if you can sidestep some of this basic human psychology. Don't fall prey to the allure of the big goal. While it may not be super-exciting to take baby steps to your destination, you must make getting there your top priority.

Look back to a big unfulfilled goal in your past. Recalling it now doesn't feel awesome, does it? It felt great to set that goal, but not achieving it hurts. You didn't consciously make it huge just so it would be harder to achieve, but you might have bitten off more than you could chew because it felt good at the time.

Don't fall into that trap again. Life isn't going to pause so that you can do this fat-loss thing. All your usual stressors, and certainly some unpredicted ones, will still be there to trip you up. Baby steps are a totally valid option, even if they aren't the most exciting one.

Chapter Forty-One
Stop Looking Back

ANOTHER THING THAT deserves a little pondering before you begin a fat-loss undertaking is the belief that the past
holds you prisoner. You have to get your past "failures" out of
your head. If you're constantly reminding yourself that you haven't
been successful in past fat-loss attempts, then you will lose that
wholly important internal locus of control that we talked about earlier. Without the belief that you are in control of your body and
that you actually can succeed, you're likely dead in the water.

The brilliant psychologist Martin Seligman studied a mental state
that he called "learned helplessness," in which a subject stops
believing she can effect change in a particular situation. He and his
colleagues experimented on dogs, using traumatic shock as a negative stimulus. When the dogs experienced a shock, they would attempt to remove the negative stimulus by escaping the source of
the shock. If the dogs were unable to escape this negative stimulus
over many repeated shocks, then they would come to the conclusion that they were helpless, and they would no longer attempt to
get away—even when escaping the shock became possible again.

Seligman found similar results in human studies in which a loud,
irritating noise was used as the negative stimulus. If the subjects
were given a means to turn off the sound, they would continue to

do so each time it happened. However, when their control over the sound was taken away, they would eventually stop trying. Then, when their control was returned and they could have turned off the noise again, they would fail to notice.

Learned helplessness is very real for many people with fat-loss goals. I've worked with plenty of women who just could not get past the past. They had allowed themselves to become scarred, and I couldn't help them get beyond the starting line. After spending a large part of their adult lives trying to lose weight through all the wrong methods, they could not truly own the idea that things would ever be different for them. They seemed to identify with the coaching I was putting before them, often remarking how "it all makes so much sense now."

Sadly, though, they had placed a permanent "fat person" label on themselves, and in the end there wasn't anything I could do to change that label in the deep recesses of their minds. Temptations were more tempting for these people than they might be for others, because somewhere in their heads that label was reminding them that they had always been fat and they always would be fat. Succumb now or later; it doesn't really matter when you *know* in your heart that trying to change is pointless.

To make things even worse, sometimes these same people seem to freeze up when certain things I ask them to do remind them of things they did out of desperation in the past. For example, if someone had been obsessed with counting every calorie she consumed, then asking her to measure her intake for just one day (if I suspected she wasn't eating enough, for example) would be enough to spin her out and remind her of all the times she suffered emotional and psychological defeat at the hands of dieting in the past.

Most of us have romantic relationships in our histories that we look back on now with a very different level of clarity than when we were in them or mourning their loss. We were smitten in every fiber of our bones and devastated when things didn't work out, but now we look back and think, "What the heck did I see in that person?" On recollection, we feel a little silly for letting ourselves get so wrapped up in something that now seems so trivial. Chances are good, though, that we never said to ourselves, "I'm terrible at relationships and will never be loved." Okay, maybe some of us said that at first, but we tend to get over that mind-set after a little time to heal.

If you think about it, your past fat-loss attempts are probably a lot like those old relationships. You didn't really know what you were doing, you let yourself believe wholeheartedly in something that was never going to work, and you took an emotional beating in the end.

Think of your past weight-loss endeavors as silly little bumps in the road. Mistakes were made, but those mistakes led to this place that you find yourself right now. You have the opportunity to have a brand-new relationship with your body—a loving, appreciative relationship in which you care for your body and it gives you access to the life you want to live.

You have done a lot of different things to try to lose weight, and all of them ended without you ever finding sustainable results. So what?

If you hold all those other attempts against yourself, as if you are somehow a loser for not succeeding at things that would have never worked anyway, then you don't stand a chance of ever really getting started with something that could actually work. You will tell yourself time and time again that failure is imminent and that the effort required for success is thereby pointless.

If you stay hung up on your past weight-loss endeavors, you might also feel guilty or remorseful for the things that you did that have had a lasting effect on your metabolism or overall health. Again, this is pointless. The past is behind you, and you aren't going to benefit by injecting negativity into the already-tough process of lifestyle change.

You are on your own unique journey unlike anyone else's. You have never failed, because that journey is still going. It's all just one big path to one destination, not a series of small battles to be won or lost. Guilt and remorse, or any other emotion based upon decisions that are long gone, have no place here.

You haven't reached the finish line yet? That doesn't matter! What matters is that you have right now, this moment, to make different choices. In fact, tomorrow doesn't matter any more than yesterday. This moment counts. And it's the only moment that counts.

"Do not dwell on the past, do not dream of the future; concentrate the mind on the present moment."
—Buddha

There's nothing in your rearview mirror worth looking at. Hopefully you learned a few things from your actions in the past, but that knowledge is with you here in the present. You can confidently look at this moment, this choice, and do what you believe is best for you based on what you currently know.

So, the next time your inner voice tries to use your past against you, saying, "You're just going to fail again," you can say, "No, you're going to fail, because your pathetic little plan to derail me isn't going to work this time."

The end of your journey may not be immediately in front of you, but I guarantee that it's not behind you.

Chapter Forty-Two
Is This a Good Time?

THUS FAR, I think I've laid down a fairly solid case for why you may have been unsuccessful in the past, as well as how you might change your head to stack the deck in your favor, but it's my hope that you'll give some serious thought to whether or not you're ready for another fat-loss attempt right now. None of the beliefs we have discussed can be ignored, but some of them might require your full attention without any of the distractions of trying to make lifestyle changes at the same time. In other words, assuming that you can change your head *while* you change your body might be a mistake.

If you currently lack self-worth or don't believe you deserve success, then you face a daily fight with your inner voice over whether or not you should be "enjoying yourself" instead of staying focused on your goals. If you are extrinsically motivated, hoping that other people will like you more if you change the way you look, then you will probably find it hard to stay on track, since you aren't really doing any of this for yourself.

We have been over all these negative beliefs, so I won't beat you over the head with each of them again, but let's add what we've learned from the transtheoretical model of change. Do you currently have what it takes to stay in the Action stage for at least six months? Be honest with yourself.

If your reasons for repeatedly returning to the Preparation stage have always been related to desperation or an emotional "need" to be thin, then you are going to have to address that if you ever hope to succeed. Likewise, if you are a self-saboteur, then starting a new plan and pretending that things will be different this time is a mistake.

At this time, can you give your goals the attention they require while simultaneously treating yourself with the respect you deserve without any further work on your perspective and beliefs?

If you can honestly answer *yes* to that question, then you're probably ready to change your lifestyle. While we're being honest, I'll tell you that very few people with a yo-yo dieting past and a history of poor body image would be able to convince me that they don't have any mental work to do before I recommend that they start any plan of mine.

Once your head is in the right place, the tangible lifestyle changes are much easier. Think about it like this: If you're doing a plan that improves health, then you'll never be physically stopped in your tracks, like when a starvation diet can't be continued forever without eventually making you too unhealthy to go on. Therefore, the reasons for quitting a healthy plan are *always* mental. Simply trying again without addressing the real reason that you quit last time will likely be unproductive and damaging to your confidence.

So I'll ask it again: What can you handle right at this moment? Where are you mentally? Are you on a time-wasting merry-go-round with your weight-loss goals? Maybe you're trying to light the wrong end of this candle.

You're just making a mess. The wick is at the other end.

Chapter Forty-Three
The Next Generation

MY GOOD FRIEND Christy handed me a photograph one day and said, "Check out this picture of me when I was 14."

"Awww," I said. "You were a cute kid."

She said, "I know. I look at that now and think I was adorable, but that's not what I thought then. I remember that moment vividly. We were on vacation in Sunriver (Oregon) and I was worried that the cellulite on my legs was going to show in the picture. Now I just wish I had known back then that I was so cute and there wasn't anything wrong with me."

Sadly, this heartbreaking tale seems to be shared by the majority of the women I have encountered in my career. It's one that says, "I just wish I could get back to that body that I had in the past, but if I'm honest with myself, I thought I was fat then, too."

Christy was trying all manner of weight-loss tricks within two years of that photograph, and unfortunately most of those tricks had a negative impact on her metabolism and actually brought about the unhealthy body that she imagined she had when she was 14. I'm happy to say that she is healthy and looks amazing today, but she suffered through most of her adult life at the hands of false beliefs that she formed in her youth.

If I were to guess, I would say that most women who read this book will be able to relate to Christy. Girls are becoming insecure about their appearance at shockingly young ages, and nobody is helping them with this nightmare. To make matters so much worse, once they believe they're flawed, virtually all of the "answers" that they stand a chance to stumble upon will be unsustainable and harmful to their health in the long run. The result is almost always a body that hoards fat whenever possible and feels awful.

I'm willing to bet that, at some point while reading this book, you've said to yourself, "Wow, I wish I knew that 20 years ago." I hear that sentiment nearly every day. Knowing what you know now, don't you agree that we have to do whatever we can to help as many girls as possible escape the torments that so many women suffer? Aren't we obligated to try to help them see their bodies in a different, more rational light?

I think it's wishful thinking to believe that we can change the whole world, but we absolutely can reach the young women we love. We can help them understand that they have the power to be healthy, that desperation isn't necessary, and that attraction is about so much more than a number on a scale. We can teach them to treat themselves with love, compassion, and patience rather than waging a war on their bodies that is fueled by desperation, loathing, and disgust.

If your relationship with your body has been a source of torment for you, then change your head and then pass on your newfound superpowers to the young women in your life. Imagine your life without all that torment. What if you could help someone else to never experience any of it? I get a lump in my throat just thinking about that.

A Plea to Mothers

Moms, it's not enough to tell your daughters that they're beautiful. They will become what you demonstrate for them. If your head is not in the right place, fine, but then you *must* hide your insecurities from your daughter at all costs!

I've seen so many situations in which moms were just absolutely blowing it with their daughters because they didn't understand the repercussions. On more than one occasion I've witnessed a young girl (under 10) take a picture of her mother with her mother's phone. Holding up the phone and smiling brightly, the child approached her mother and said, "Look, Mommy, I took a picture of you." The mother snatched the phone from the child's hands, deleting the picture as quickly as possible, saying, "Don't do that! Mommy looks gross! You don't need to be taking pictures of me!"

The results were the same each time. The child would look hurt and thoughtful as she tried to process what had just happened. If I could have read her mind, I know she was thinking, "I don't understand. I was so proud because I took a picture of the most beautiful person in the whole world, but Mommy got mad at me for it. Why doesn't Mommy think she's beautiful?"

And then the searching begins. That child has been set on a course that will lead to her eventually finding out what her mother doesn't like about herself. Then she will look to her own body to see if those things are wrong with her, too.

Someday she'll mention those insecurities to the woman who gave them to her, and her mother won't have a clue how to respond except to say, "Oh, honey, you're beautiful." But of course the daughter already knows that her mom can't be trusted. After all, Mom was beautiful all those years ago, too, but she didn't believe it, so why would she be right about her daughter?

Things get worse when moms pass on their curses to their daughters more directly. When a daughter complains about a particular part of her body, some mothers will say things like, "You just have the Jones butt." Or, "Yep, you inherited the Smith thighs." This is like saying, "Here you go, sweetie. These are the self-judgments that have plagued me my whole life. They're yours now. Take good care of them, and in return they'll always make you miserable."

If you have already passed some of these things on to your daughter, you don't have time to feel bad about it. The race is on! You must get your own head on the right path and then start talking to her about these issues as often as possible. Tell her how you've been wrong for your whole life. Tell her that you overlooked so much truth in favor of assumptions and negative emotions. Tell her that you're better now than ever before and you're getting even better all the time. If she's old enough, ask her to read this book. Whatever you do, you *must* act! The alternative is to sit back, believing that there's no hope, and watch her travel the same road as you. All the heartache, sadness, depression, frustration, and anger that you experienced will be her inheritance.

Just talk to her.

A Plea to Fathers

If you've read this far, the odds are high that you're not a man (kudos to any man who did). However, I need to write this one small section to the fathers out there. If you have a daughter, maybe you can ask her father to read this. Tell him I tried to keep it brief.

Gentlemen, we have a huge responsibility as the fathers of daughters. Girls need their daddies. The relationships we forge with our little girls are precious and too important to ever accurately put into words, but I'm going to give it a shot.

It's easy to get caught up in the day-to-day grind of our provider instincts. We go out into the world with motives that sometimes aren't quite understood by the women in our lives. Striving is in our nature. It's a testosterone thing, and it isn't going away.

However, we can't forget that our daughters are always watching and that they will use what they see in us as the template by which they'll measure other men. As such, we can't let them down.

You may not always understand when the women around you suffer through angst and frustration about their bodies. Their self-sabotaging behavior and perfectionism might not make sense to you, but you can absolutely see that it isn't fun for them. They suffer in ways that we just don't. The good news is that you can be a massive influence in your daughter's life, an influence that could help her escape all that suffering.

To show her what she needs to know to be healthy and happy, you have to show her what a good man really is. Love the hell out of her mother. Show your daughter that you deeply respect her mom. You can't afford to hide your emotions in front of your little girl, or she'll grow up and find a man who doesn't express himself to her. In a relationship like that, her inner voice will be free to run her into the ground as she tries to figure out what he's thinking. She deserves better.

Show her, too, that all women deserve respect. Don't ever let her see you ogle a woman who's not her mother. I'm by no means saying that you have to stop being a man. Most of us will never be able to stop ourselves from glancing at beauty when we encounter it, but anything that looks like lust will be recorded by your little girl, and she will use the image of the women you ogle as a reference when she forms her own beliefs about how she should look. The world will bombard her with enough of that, and she doesn't need it from the most important man in her young life.

Some of us are not great communicators, but that can't be your excuse for not talking to your daughter. She absolutely *is* a communicator. Even if she's shy or introverted, she will likely need lots of communication from those she loves. She needs affirmation. She needs affection. And she needs you to get to know her on a deep, emotional level so that she can understand how men think. If you remain mysterious, she'll jump to conclusions to fill in what she doesn't know about men.

If you show her what a good man is, she won't enter the dating world feeling like men are horrible creatures who want only one thing from her. While it may be tempting to tell her that boys are all pigs when you're trying to protect her in her youth, it's much more effective to teach her to make good decisions. *Be* a great man in her life, and she will pick a great man to replace you. I agree that the thought of being replaced is enough to make our knees weak, but seeing her in a loving relationship with a respectable young man will be a wonderful reward for all your hard work.

We've got this. We can raise daughters who love themselves. We only have to do what comes naturally to us and remember that they are the reason why we get out of bed in the morning.

Chapter Forty-Four
Those Who Have Gone Before

I KNOW THAT many of the changes I'm proposing sound impossible, but I assure you that I've seen them come to fruition. I asked a few of the women I've worked with to share their experiences with you so that you might hear, in their own words, that change is possible.

<u>Kate</u>

Body image issues have been a part of my life for as long as I can remember—meaning from around fourth or fifth grade (about 9 years old) on up. Where and why it started, of course, is due to many different reasons and circumstances. The women in my life growing up were always unhappy with their bodies, doing diets all the time, disparaging themselves in the mirror, etc., and when I looked at those women in my life who were my role models, I felt "less than" them because, if they thought they were fat, then I must be really disgusting! I was put on diets at a young age and told that my knee problems were due to weight—even though in reality I was not a huge girl.

Then bring on the girls at school who were also coming from homes where what you look like is important (standing in the school bathroom analyzing flaws together was not uncommon), combine this with media pressure and magazines telling girls how they should look and how to obtain that look, and not a single argument from the other side about how it was all bullcrap to begin with. No one ever said, "Focus on being healthy and strong, and the best version of you will shine through." No one, not a single person in my life, showed me a healthy way to be a whole woman who loved herself enough to be healthy both in mind and body. It makes me sad to think about all these women, because now I know they are/were in the same mental prison as me. It is debilitating and a terrible cycle to be trapped in.

When I came stumbling into your gym four years ago, I was in a state of grief over many family losses (so I was under an incredible amount of emotional stress). I was dealing with a very strong-willed and intense child, my husband's job was incredibly stressful, and I was desperate for something to make me feel better about life—which at that time meant feeling better about my body and how it looked in the mirror. I have learned that the more stress I'm under in other areas in my life, the worse the body-image monster and insecurity in my self-worth becomes. At the time I was unable to get the monster under control.

I believed that if I just felt better about what I saw in the mirror, then it would make those other things in my life somehow less bad. In retrospect that is so silly, but at the time it was all-consuming. These thought processes impacted everything. I was constantly telling myself how ugly, fat, and gross I was—if only I could lose ten pounds I would be happy; other people would accept me better; I would be enough for myself and others. Over the years I've asked myself why I think these things about myself or why I can't just stop thinking that way. A solid answer or change never came from asking why, and it became even more frustrating because I would feel like a failure because I couldn't make the tape in my head stop playing negativity.

Then, after being at your gym for a little more than two years with no change in how I was feeling about myself, you took the time to stop me mid-set because I had cringed at a picture of myself. (Avoiding being in pictures so that I wouldn't have to analyze all my flaws was a big part of my life.) You simply said, "What has happened to you that made you think this way?"

I don't know what happened, but I went home and that "what" question nagged at me. I sat down and wrote five pages of things that I could remember that were still with me—painful things that helped shape my current state. Just getting them down on paper was the start to releasing those things and the grip they held on me. I gave you the paper—nervous as hell for anyone else to read it—and you simply and rationally walked me through those things and showed me which were valid and which weren't, and for those things that were valid, why I didn't have to take those opinions as truth anymore. You will never know how much that impacted my life. I was able to let go of so much junk, like a weight lifted off of me. I had been carrying a bunch of other people's opinions (both real and perceived) of myself and not my own truth.

I then had to start the hard work of changing those voices in my head from the ones I had carried for 30 years to new, truthful, real ones based on my own view. It was not at all easy, but I had to do it for myself and for my daughter, who was 7 at the time. There was no way I wanted her to grow up with the same sort of internal torment I lived with. I had done a good job of being aware enough of my problem to know that I didn't want to pass it on, so I would never say anything about my body in front of her or let her see me criticize myself. But there were other things I know she saw that I'm not proud of, like how I would duck out of pictures or not wear a certain thing and come up with an excuse for it. I knew I had to get better. I had to change for both of us and even for the girls that would be her friends in the future—I wanted to be the role model I never had.

I started literally telling myself good things when I looked in the mirror. It felt ridiculous, but I did it anyway. I also meditated, which does not come easily for me, but I truly believe it helped me become more aware and let me catch myself when the negative tape would begin to play in my head. When I would be in a room with a woman I felt less than because of what her body looked like (this used to destroy me, and I would go into a cocoon), I would catch myself and tell myself that I am enough, I am strong, healthy, smart, and beautiful, and so is that woman, and it's okay. Actually, it was more than okay, because this is how women should try to treat one another: build each other up instead of comparing and tearing ourselves and each other down. This was huge for me, because it played into social issues that had plagued me forever as well.

As my brain changed, everything changed. I was no longer going to the gym in order to pay my debt for what I thought I had eaten wrong or in order to make myself look better. I was going to the gym because I valued my health and I wanted to become the best version of myself for not only me, but also my daughter. I wanted to break the cycle so she could live in this new freedom I had found. And now that I was going to the gym for the right reasons, I got stronger faster, food didn't hold the emotional grip on me anymore, and I began to lose fat where it plagued me the most, a happy side effect to getting my brain realigned. Not only did it impact my physical life, but I also finally felt "good enough" to pursue what I had dreamed about for a long time: putting myself out there as a photographer and starting my own business.

When I had been battling the body-image monsters, I never felt good enough in so many areas of my life, and it is pervasive how it impacts everything. This was such a huge deal. I was putting my art out there to be judged by other people I had no control over. This is something I had intentionally avoided at all costs, because being judged by others was horrifying. I was judging myself so harshly already that I couldn't bear to hear it from other people. But, after putting in the work to rewire my brain, I truly didn't care what anyone else would think. I loved to take pictures, and I just did it.

Has the journey been easy-breezy since the first "aha" moment? No. I'm almost two years in and still making progress. I still battle the monster in my head, but I now catch it when it first starts up and tell it where to go jump, if you know what I mean. I still find it is worse if I am under stress in other areas of my life, but that realization is in itself a victory because knowing is half the battle.

I guess that's my journey in a not-so-nutshell.

<u>Jeni</u>

"I've been a yo-yo dieter for years, but I have the heart of an overeater! I would do things like SlimFast, Weight Watchers, and then Beach Body with *crazy* amounts of gym time, always with that desperate desire to be a certain size. But this time it's different! I realize that it isn't a sprint, and quite frankly it isn't even a marathon. This is life, and health is now my goal. When I make a less-than-stellar food choice, or when I miss a lifting session because my 2-year-old is plastered to my side, I don't freak out! I take a deep breath, be in this moment, and choose better in the next moment. A healthy body is what I'm after: to run and play with my kids and to be around a long time for them.

I'd like to add that this mind shift is a journey. It's not like my mind suddenly changed overnight. I still have to repeat the truth to myself and be mindful in each moment so the crazy voice of this world stays drowned out. I have become so much kinder to myself. I used to expect perfection and berate myself when I wasn't perfect. I'm learning to accept what is, change what I can, but allow myself the freedom to take this journey—not to just be there. I like this new version of me! I'm happy, and I'm kind, and I laugh a lot more.

Jason, I can't say thank you enough! You have given me the tools to be successful and to keep my mind in the right spot!"

Kristin

"The absolute best part for me has been the shift in mentality. I cannot explain why or how it happened, but since I was 12 years old I struggled with body-image issues and food compulsions. I no longer have food compulsions, and I never even think about my body size anymore. I'm only sad that I wasted 30-plus years not living like this before; it took so much of my energy.

The best part is that, because of this shift in mentality, I'm confident that I will not gain any of my weight back (I went from a size 14 to a size 8). My energy is great, and my relationships are better. My parents are both morbidly obese, and my brother is getting close, and at one point I thought that might be in the cards for me as well.

I'm pretty sure sugar and grains had been a part of my food compulsions, but the daily meditation, nine hours of sleep a night, massive amounts of walking, and moderate lifting have been a game-changer for me.

In the past, I would go on diets and white-knuckle it the whole time. Now I eat until satiety three times a day and no longer live with the guilt and shame that I used to feel after stuffing myself (I would overeat all the time, and that no longer happens).

I plan to stick with this for life. I no longer think about it—it's just what I do!"

Chapter Forty-Five
Epilogue: So...What Happens Now?

IF I'VE DONE my job, then your relationship with your body is already forever changed in some small way. It's my hope that you'll take what you learned here and do the work of changing in big ways.

What you have that you may not have always known about are choices. You can choose to become someone who loves herself through and through. You can choose to end the war with your body and extend an olive branch. I'm not talking about the nebulous kind of choices in which you simply tell yourself that things will be different from now on. I'm talking about getting down to business, nose to the grindstone, and working hard to become a new, healthier version of yourself, beginning with the gray stuff between your ears.

If the majority of your problems with your body originate in your own mind, then you aren't a victim; you were simply misinformed. Yes, a lifetime of living with one inner voice can leave scars and deep-seated beliefs about your world, but you still hold the reins.

So what are you going to do? How badly do you want relief from those negative thoughts and emotions? I've done my best to dismantle every destructive belief you might hold about your body, but this is where we must part ways. The path before you is a hard one, but you're not the first to traverse it. Many have gone before you to that happier place in their own minds, where life is a series of experiences unhampered by the constant weight of dissatisfaction with their bodies. There are no superheroes in that land. Just regular folks who accomplished something that anyone can.

Will change be easy? Hell, no! Will it be worth it? Abso-freaking-lutely! Can you *really* do it? Don't be silly. Of course you can.

Go forth and be awesome.